Treasures of the
Series Three: Cultural Memory
Volume 7

Mary Boyle, Philip Flacke,
Timothy Powell

Epic!
Homer and the *Nibelungenlied* in Translation

Editor: Henrike Lähnemann

Taylor Institution Library, Oxford, 2024

 **TAYLOR INSTITUTION LIBRARY**
St Giles, Oxford, OX1 3NA

https://www.bodleian.ox.ac.uk/libraries/taylor/exhibitions-and-publications

© 2024 The Authors

Some rights are reserved. This book is made available under the Creative Commons Attribution-Non-Commercial-No Derivative Works 4.0 International (CC BY 4.0). This license allows for copying any part of the work for personal and non-commercial use, providing author attribution is clearly stated.

Digital downloads for this volume are available at https://historyofthebook.mml.ox.ac.uk/epic-homer-and-nibelungenlied-in-translation/
They include a pdf ebook of the text and an expanded exhibition catalogue.

The cover image features the woodcut illustration for the first 'Abenteuer' of *Das Nibelungenlied* in the translation by Gotthard Oswald Marbach based on a drawing by Julius Hübner, published as monument for the centenary celebration for printing, *Denkmal zur vierten Säcularfeier der Buchdruckerkunst*, Leipzig 1840.

Catalogue accompanying the exhibition 'Epic! Homer and the *Nibelungenlied* in Translation' in the Voltaire Room of the Taylor Institution Library, Oxford 22 May to 13 June 2024.

Typesetting by Henrike Lähnemann
Cover design by Emma Huber

ISBN 978-1-8384641-8-9

Printed in the United Kingdom and United States by Lightning Source for Taylor Institution Library

Table of Contents

HENRIKE LÄHNEMANN – Preface	v
JOHN BUTCHER – Introduction	vii
PHILIP FLACKE – The *Nibelungenlied* as 'German *Iliad*'	1
Appendix: 'A German *Iliad*'. Endorsements and Critique	5
MARY BOYLE – The Victorian *Nibelungenlied*	14
Epic Adaptations for Children	20
TIMOTHY POWELL – The *Nibelungenlied* from National Socialist Epic to Socialist National Epic	24
Appendix: Epic Beginnings	
Iliad	40
Odyssey	44
Nibelungenlied	47

Exhibition Catalogue

Taylorian: Epic! Homer and the *Nibelungenlied* in Translation
    curated by MARY BOYLE and PHILIP FLACKE

Section 1: Epic?	50
Section 2: Translating Epic Verse	55
Section 3: Mapping Myth	59
Section 4: Powerful Women	64
Section 5: The Pierced Body	69
Section 6: Violent Revenge	75

Bodleian Library: Homeric Fragments
    curated by NIGEL WILSON and PETER TÓTH   82

Illustration 1: The statues above the entrance to the Taylorian representing languages taught in Oxford in the 19th century. Photograph: Henrike Lähnemann

Introduction xiii

Nagel aufgehankht und wie der edele Siffrid der anderen Nacht Brunehilden bezwang mit hartem Khampfe das sie Günthern zu willen geworden' ('How King Gunther of Burgundy upon his wedding night on the Rhine desired to sleep with Brünhild of Isenstein and how she tied up his hands and feet and hung him up on a nail and how the gallant Siegfried the following night compelled Brünhild in a violent struggle to give in to Gunther's will'). A full transcription of Mohr's annotations may be found in Jürgen Rabe, *Die Sprache der Berliner Nibelungenlied-Handschrift J (Ms. germ. Fol. 474)*, Göppingen, Alfred Kümmerle, 1972, pp. 250-252.

Illustration 6: The palas of Obermontani Castle. Photograph: John Butcher

*Illustration 7: Books in the exhibition from the Taylorian collection.
Photograph: Philip Flacke*

xii *John Butcher*

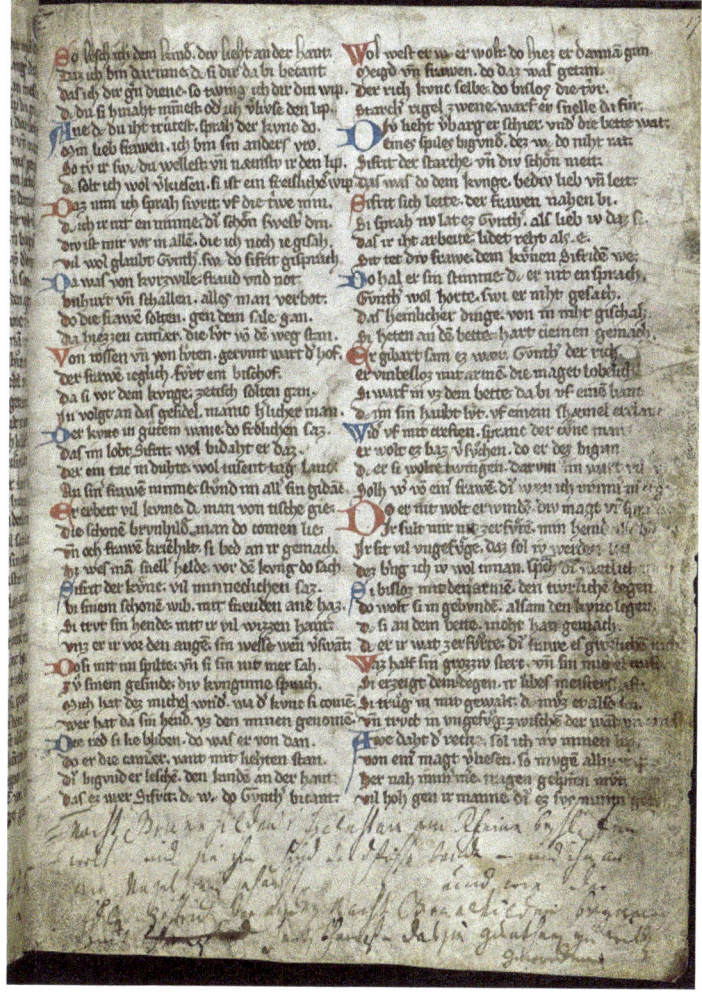

Illustration 5: Berlin, Staatsbibliothek, Germ. Fol. 474 (ms. I), fol. 17r.

The strophes correspond to 651-670 of the Codex Sangallensis 857 (ms. B) and belong to the tenth *aventiure* of Brünhild's reception in Worms. The addition at the bottom of the page was penned by Count Karl Mohr who introduced into the Obermontani manuscript, which at the time belonged to him, several annotations, dating them Latsch, 22 July 1797. The annotation appearing on 17r, which continues from 16v, reads as follows: '[*Wie Khonig Günther von Burgund die feste=*]*=nacht Brunehilden von Iselnstain am Rheine beschlafen wolt und sie ihm Händ und Füsse bande – und ihn an ain*

Introduction xi

Illustration 4: Obermontani castle. Photograph: John Butcher

Obermontani Castle is located above the town of Latsch in the lower Vinschgau (South Tyrol), at the entrance to the Martelltal. It was built by Albert of Tyrol in 1228 in order to counterbalance the weight of the Diocese of Chur. From 1300 onwards, it belonged to the lords of Montani, who during the Fifteenth century significantly enlarged the premises. Later, as the lords of Montani became extinct, the castle passed into the hands of the counts of Mohr who presumably stored there the renowned library once owned by the local intellectual Anton von Annenberg (1427/1428-1483) and consisting of around 250 volumes. In 1833, after the death of the last of the Mohrs, the castle fell rapidly into disrepair and its marbles were plundered by greedy farmers. All that remains today is a ruin currently closed to the public. There is good reason to believe that ms. I of the *Nibelungenlied* was kept in one of the rooms of the palas (residential quarters) and that Beda Weber unearthed it there in 1834. The somewhat spartan interior, without any traces of previous mural paintings, is offset by impressive brickwork and windows providing stunning views over the Alpine landscape of the Vinschgau.

will survey Ernest Reyer's *Sigurd* (1884), a hybrid opera mixing the *Nibelungenlied* and Wagner's *Ring des Nibelungen*, and Hélène Cixous' subtle and profoundly poetic tragedy *L'Histoire (qu'on ne connaîtra jamais)* (1994). A final conference will be meeting further afield in Trieste and setting out to consider the theory of diachronic translation by way of the *Nibelungenlied*: amongst other features, it will have the honour of presenting the first Slovenian translation of the German epic, composed by Simon Širca.

The research and educational project at the Meran Academy *"Da brachte man die Märe in andrer Könge Land". Europäische Überlieferung und Strahlkraft des* Nibelungenliedes / *La fortuna europea del* Cantare dei Nibelunghi, also including school visits throughout South Tyrol, individual history lectures, book presentations, a cultural evening in Latsch and the four-part lecture series *Das* Nibelungenlied *und…*, forms part of a considerably larger initiative, NIBELUNGEN. Die Rückkehr. Il ritorno, organised in association with Kunst Meran and its dynamic director Martina Oberprantacher. The latter institution is currently playing host to an exhibition curated by Harald F. Theiss: *Imagine Worlds*. The centrepiece of this exhibition is the Obermontani manuscript, which Berlin's Staatsbibliothek has most kindly lent for the occasion, thus allowing it to return to that Alpine region in whose castles it was preserved for at least three and a half centuries (c. 1472–1834).

The Reading and Reception of the Homeric Poems and the Nibelungenlied *in Germany and Europe from the Eighteenth Century to the Present* constitutes an integral part of the Meran project. I am grateful to Nigel Wilson for having broadened the initiative to the University of Oxford and to Henrike Lähnemann for having guided the event into the exceptionally rich and multi-faceted programme of Oxford Medieval Studies.

Gargazon (South Tyrol), 5 May 2024,
John Butcher

dering Vinschgau, delved into the complex personality of Beda Weber, that Benedictine monk and scholar who in 1834 discovered in Obermontani Castle, buried beneath rags and other rubbish, the parchment ms. I of the *Nibelungenlied*: he acquired the priceless artefact for the princely sum of 10 florins, today the equivalent of a few hundred pounds. A third conference in South Tyrol's capital Bozen, planned by the local Società Dante Alighieri, compared and contrasted the two poetic masterpieces of the Italian and German Middle Ages, the *Divine Comedy* and the *Nibelungenlied*, highlighting similarities and differences in the portrayal of specific characters; extracts from Dante's poem and the *Nibelungenlied* were read in the original Italian and Middle High German by Marta Penchini and myself. A fourth conference took place in the magnificent setting of Villa Vigoni on Lake Como and revolved around the arrival of the Nibelungs in Italy: the first event of its sort ever to take place, it opened with a paper by the pioneer in the field, Verio Santoro, and moved freely from Giosue Carducci's verses to Italian parodies of Wagner's tetralogy and comics.

Illustration 3: Meran Academy. Photograph: Meran Academy

Forthcoming events comprise a large-scale conference on the European reception of the medieval poem, due to be held at the Academy, with papers on Denmark, Holland, Hungary, Ukraine, the United Kingdom, Greece and other nations: a paper on France, for example,

JOHN BUTCHER
Introduction

The Meran Academy, founded in 1949 and celebrating this year its seventy-fifth anniversary, is a non-profit association whose goal is to foster cultural and scientific ties between the German- and Italian-speaking areas. In the past decade, its research and educational projects have been focused to a considerable degree on the European reception of literary classics such as Dante's *Commedia*, Ariosto's *Orlando Furioso* and Tasso's *Gerusalemme Liberata*. Its most recent initiative switches to a classic of German poetry, the anonymous medieval epic entitled *Nibelungenlied*, circulating widely from somewhere around 1200 onwards.

Taking its cue from a *Nibelungenlied* manuscript once housed in Obermontani Castle in the nearby town of Latsch (Vinschgau), the multilingual research and educational project *"Da brachte man die Märe in andrer Könge Land". Europäische Überlieferung und Strahlkraft des* Nibelungenliedes */ La fortuna europea del* Cantare dei Nibelunghi, coordinated by Verena Pohl alongside Federica Gazzani, provides a wide-ranging series of conferences and lectures within the Meran Academy. Further events taking place in South Tyrol, Italy and England, hosted by partner institutions, aim to widen the scope of the project, exploring lesser-known facets of the reception of the *Nibelungenlied*.

An initial conference in Meran investigated the manuscript tradition of the *Nibelungenlied*, including an analysis of the variants of the Obermontani manuscript (ms. I) compared to the text of Codex Sangallensis 857 (ms. B), as well as a discussion of the Ambraser Heldenbuch (ms. d), produced in South Tyrol by Hans Ried from Bozen by order of Emperor Maximilian I himself. A second conference in Marienberg Abbey, on the western border of South Tyrol's mean-

*Illustration 2: The poster by the Meran Academy for the event.
Design: Meran Academy*

The new introductory essay by Philip Flacke discusses the trope of the 'German *Iliad*' which is so ubiquitous that we have dedicated one of the appendices to a survey of its appearance in literature. It starts with the first editions of both the Homeric and medieval epic texts and their inculturation into a history of the German nation – something that all subsequent adaptations have to grapple with. This is particularly striking in the third essay by Timothy Powell who highlights how the GDR appropriated (with difficulties!) the *Nibelungenlied* which had been tainted by National Socialism. Taken together, the three essays follow the stages of (re-)discovery of the *Nibelungenlied* from the 18th century, focussing on the aspect of reading it as national epos and, to this end, linking it with longer established icons of epic literature, most prominently Homer's *Iliad* and *Odyssey*.

The centre of the book is the exhibition catalogue which combines precious first editions of translations of the 18th and 19th centuries with cheap popular adaptations particularly for children. The exhibition builds on the Taylorian collection, supplemented from Bodleian holdings and private loans from the organisers – it took us all by surprise how much relevant epic material was amongst the formative books on our shelves!

We are grateful to all who helped make this exhibition and catalogue happen: Emma Huber, the librarians and interns at the Taylorian; Thomas Wood and other helpful proofreaders in Oxford and beyond; all contributors to the workshop 'The Reading and Reception of the Homeric Poems and the *Nibelungenlied* in Germany and Europe from the Eighteenth Century to the Present'; above all for the initiative and the support to the Meran Academy, particularly John Butcher, who coordinated the European-wide project – now more important than ever!

Oxford, 15 May 2024
Henrike Lähnemann for the organisers and authors

Henrike Lähnemann
Preface

The exhibition 'Epic! Homer and the *Nibelungenlied* in Translation' accompanies the workshop 'The Reading and Reception of the Homeric Poems and the *Nibelungenlied* in Germany and Europe from the Eighteenth Century to the Present'. Both build on one of the founding principles of the Taylor Institution Library: to chart the development of 'Nationalliteratur' in the context of 'Weltliteratur'. The four figures standing proud over the St Giles entrance of the building represent French, German, Italian, and Spanish literature as a group of women, collectively fighting, scattering a cornucopia, enlightening, and, last but not least, thinking. The library itself was founded in the 19th century, at the time of establishing the 'canon' of German literature, dedicated to making texts in their original form available to students, starting with incunables and going to the newest contemporary literature.

This book and exhibition stand at the intersection of two larger projects: that of the year-long celebration of the legacy of the *Nibelungenlied* by the Meran Academy (more on that later by its organiser John Butcher); and that of the 'Cultural Memory' series of the 'Treasures of the Taylorian'. The latter is dedicated to uncovering hidden connections between collections of the Taylorian and wider topics and issues, for example between the Reformation pamphlets held by the library and Expressionist art (volume 5), or between book layout and multilingual writing (volume 2).

In 2022, Mary Boyle organised an exhibition 'Violent Victorian Medievalism' which turned into volume 4 of the series. Her essay focussing on the representation of women, heroes and violence in English *Nibelungenlied* adaptations has been combined with her discussion of how to translate violence for children into one of the three introductory essays of this book.

PHILIP FLACKE
The *Nibelungenlied* as 'German *Iliad*'

If you had been a child at a German secondary school in the latter half of the nineteenth century, you might well have been asked to write an essay on the following question (as suggested for this purpose in an 1879 collection of possible topics): 'Can the *Nibelungenlied* and *Gudrun* rightly be called the German *Iliad* and *Odyssey*?'[1] Or, if you had been an American child in the US, you might have had to read about Siegfried and Kriemhilda in a school book entitled *The Story of the German Iliad* from 1892.[2] By this time, the idea of likening the *Nibelungenlied* to Homer's *Iliad* (and sometimes the *Kudrun*, the other great thirteenth-century German epic, to Homer's *Odyssey*) had been a well-established trope for over a century. How did it come about? What role does it play that it can be found in a school setting? And what does it actually signify to call the *Nibelungenlied* a 'German *Iliad*'?

Both the modern reception of the *Nibelungenlied* and the German Grecophilia that would go on to influence Goethe and the bourgeoisie of the nineteenth century, can be argued to have a common starting point: the year 1755.[3] In Dresden, Johann Joachim Winckelmann published his *Thoughts on the Imitation of Greek Works in Painting and the Art of Sculpture* inviting his German readers to identify with the people of Homer and to follow their example. At the same time, the German physician Jacob Hermann Obereit uncovered what was to be known as the Donaueschingen manuscript C of

---

[1] 'Verdienen Nibelungenlied und Gudrun mit Recht die deutsche Ilias und Odyssee genannt zu werden?' Hermann Kluge, *Themata zu deutschen Aufsätzen und Vorträgen, für höhere Unterrichtsanstalten* (Altenburg ²1879), p. 29.

[2] Mary E. Burt, *The Story of the German Iliad, A School Reader for the Sixth and Seventh Grades* (New York 1892).

[3] E.g. Joachim Heinzle, *Die Nibelungen, Lied und Sage* (Darmstadt 2005), pp. 109–10. A comprehensive bibliography of the reception of the *Nibelungenlied* with a wealth of other resources on https://www.nibelungenrezeption.de/

the *Nibelungenlied* in a palace library in Vorarlberg after the text had almost been forgotten in the sixteenth and seventeenth centuries. Obereit informed the Swiss critic Johann Jakob Bodmer about his find, who then went on to publish part of the text both in Middle High German and in translation. Bodmer had already influenced a new perception of Homer in the German speaking world.[4] On encounter with the *Nibelungenlied*, he recognised something in it that reminded him of the Homeric epics, especially the *Iliad*. Bodmer's publications on the subject can be seen as an ongoing project of 'Homerising' the *Nibelungenlied*, of assimilating it to his ideas of the Ancient Greek epics. His impulse of looking at the medieval epic through the eyes of Homer provided a starting point for a shared reception of these texts and the stories they tell.

For Bodmer and his contemporaries, connecting to the epic texts – and making connections between them – was in many ways a question of metrics. The quest for the German hexameter occupied writers from different generations, some of whom contributed passages from both *Iliad* and *Odyssey* in periodicals for public assessment.[5] Not only was the *Nibelungenlied* adapted in the metre of Homer on three different occasions Homer was translated into German in ways that imitated the form of the *Nibelungenlied*.[6]

---

[4] Annegret Pfalzgraf, *Eine Deutsche Ilias? Homer und das 'Nibelungenlied' bei Johann Jakob Bodmer. Zu den Anfängen der nationalen Nibelungenrezeption im 18. Jahrhundert* (Marburg 2003), pp. 7–60; Günter Häntzschel, 'Der deutsche Homer vom 16. bis zum 19. Jahrhundert' in *Übersetzung, Translation, Traduction, Ein internationales Handbuch zur Übersetzungsforschung*, vol. 3 (Berlin and Boston 2011), pp. 2423–27, here p. 2424; Sotera Fornaro, 'Homer in der deutschen Literatur' in *Homer-Handbuch. Leben, Werk, Wirkung* (Stuttgart and Weimar 2011), pp. 358–70, here p. 359.

[5] Günter Häntzschel, 'Die Ausbildung der deutschen Literatursprache des 18. Jahrhunderts durch Übersetzungen. Homer-Verdeutschungen als produktive Kraft' in *Mehrsprachigkeit in der deutschen Aufklärung* (Hamburg 1985), pp. 117–32.

[6] By Ferdinand Wilhelm Karl Rinne in 1860 (*Iliad*), by Ernst Johann Jakob Engel in 1885 (*Odyssey*), and by Julius Schultz in 1901 (*Iliad*). Cf. Hans-Joachim Jakob, 'Deutsche Homer-Übersetzungen seit der frühen Neuzeit. Bibliographische Übersicht' in *Homer und die deutsche Literatur* (München 2010), pp. 290–98.

Making the *Nibelungenlied* a 'German *Iliad*' was always a political enterprise. Annegret Pfalzgraf has shown that already in the Seven Years' War, shortly after its resurfacing in Vorarlberg, a patriotic agenda played a role in how the story of Siegfried and Kriemhild was talked about.[7] Carlyle later claimed the *Nibelungenlied* for 'us English teutones'.[8] Its nationalist and antisemitic reception culminated in the years when 'Dolchstoß' and 'Nibelungentreue' entered the language of the Third Reich, but does not end in 1945.

Violence and war are prevailing topics of all three epics – as is sex. Nevertheless, and sometimes no doubt partly because of their militaristic appeal, the stories have often been told to children. Again, it is worthwhile to ask why and how this was done and to look at parallels in the reception. Such popular retellings often do not limit themselves to the *Nibelungenlied*, but merge different texts and subjects including Old Norse literature or even Wagner, thus constructing a homogenous 'Germanic' mythology that is ultimately a product of the eighteenth and nineteenth centuries.

Aiming at younger readers or wider audiences, a number of writers published accounts of the lives of both Siegfried *and* the Homeric heroes. Gustav Schwab, famous for his *Gods and Heroes: Myths and Epics of Ancient Greece* (*Die schönsten Sagen des klassischen Alterthums*, 1838–40), had first written a different book that started with the story of the Horned Siegfried ('Der gehörnte Siegfried' in *Buch der schönsten Geschichten und Sagen*, also under the title *Die deutschen Volksbücher*, 1836–37). Helene Otto published versions of the *Odyssey*, the *Iliad*, and *Die Nibelungen* in the language of ten-year-olds (1903/04). The German author Franz Fühmann adapted both the *Nibelungenlied* (in 1971 and 1973) and the Homeric epics (numerous times). Anglophone authors like Padraic Colum (*The Adventure of Odysseus* 1918, *The Children of Odin* 1920) and Barbara Leonie Picard (*The Odyssey of Homer* 1952, *German Hero-Sagas and Folk-Tales* 1958, *The Iliad of Homer* 1960) likewise published children's books

---

[7] Cf. Pfalzgraf, *Eine Deutsche Ilias?*, pp. 118–136.
[8] In 1831. Cf. Mary Boyle's essay in this book.

on both Greek and 'Germanic' mythology. Sometimes, such accounts appeared as part of the same series, as in the case of the books entitled *Told to the Children*, which are part of the exhibition.

While academic translations were historically monopolised by men, a substantial part of children's books on Homer and the Nibelungen were contributed by women. Today, we witness a trend in literary retellings of myth, often written from feminist perspectives. Being intensely discussed on BookTok and other social media, these accounts do not limit themselves to children's literature. Especially in the anglophone world, various writers are following earlier examples of novels by Mary Renault, Margaret Atwood, Madeline Miller, and others, focusing on women and marginalised voices, and rereading Homer from queer and postcolonial perspectives.[9] The *Nibelungenlied*, too, has in the last years prompted contemporary reimaginings by writers like Ulrike Draesner and Felicitas Hoppe. The reception of Homer and the Nibelungen is very much a matter of today.

The exhibition reveals the different stages and trends, the key impulses, and some idiosyncratic approaches to the translation and adaption of the *Iliad*, the *Odyssey*, and the *Nibelungenlied*. It showcases material from the Taylor Institution Library's collections, alongside additions from the Bodleian Library and some items on private loan. Building on the 2022 exhibition 'Violent Victorian Medievalism', curated by Mary Boyle, it shines particular light on adaptations for children and to the fraught topic of women and violence. The books featured tell the story of the various attempts to assert ownership of these epics. This was not simply a matter of translating the texts, but of claiming them for different national and pre-national identities, for specific ideas of masculinity and femininity, and for militaristic agendas and racist ideologies. But also, more recently, the epics have been retold with feminist, queer, and anti-colonial causes in mind. Maybe that can be the subject for another exhibition.

---

[9] For postcolonial perspectives cf. Emily Greenwood, 'Postcolonial Perceptions of Homeric Epic' in *The Cambridge Guide to Homer* (Cambridge 2020), pp. 532–35.

Appendix: 'A German *Iliad*' Endorsements and Critique

Es ist eine Art von Ilias, und wenigstens etwas, so die Grundlage einer Ilias in sich enthält.

> Bodmer in a letter to his friend Laurenz Zellweger (24 August 1755), shortly after getting to know the *Nibelungenlied*.

Dieses Gedicht hat etwas iliadisches, dem an der Vollkommenheit, die in der Epopöe erfordert wird, nicht viel abgehet.

> Bodmer (?) 1757 in an announcement of the upcoming partial edition of the *Nibelungenlied* (*Freymüthige Nachrichten*, pp. 74–75).

Alle diese Stücke habe ich abgeschnitten, und ich glaube mit demselben Rechte, mit welchem Homer die Entführung der Helena, die Aufopferung der Iphigenia, und alle Begegnisse der zehn Jahre, die vor dem Zwiste zwischen Achilles und Agamemnon vorhergegangen sind, weggelassen hat, auf die er nur bey Gelegenheiten sich als auf bekannte Sachen beziehet.

> Bodmer in the preface to his partial *Nibelungenlied* edition *Chriemhilden Rache, Und Die Klage. Zwey Heldengedichte Aus dem schvväbischen Zeitpuncte* (1757), p. VII.

Die Dapferkeit erscheint hier in einer wunderbaren Verschiedenheit bey verschiedenen Personen; eine andere ist Rüdegers, eine andere Blödelins, eine andere Hagenen, des Volkers, Dieterichs von Bern – In der Beschreibung der Kämpfe herrschet eine Mannigfaltigkeit von Begegnissen, so daß schwerlich ein Kampf, ein Gefecht, dem andern gleich ist. Jedes neue Gefecht erhebt sich über das vorhergehende an Grösse, Gefahr, und Verwirrung. – Das sind Eigenschaften, die sonst dem Homer zugehören. Der Poet hat auch dieses mit dem Griechen mehr als so mancher anderer Poet gemein, daß er uns selten an den Poeten gedenken läßt; er nimmt uns allein mit seiner Handlung ein, und machet uns aus Lesern zu Hörern.

> Bodmer in the preface to his partial *Nibelungenlied* edition (1757), pp. VII–VIII.

Die Klage ist ein besonderes Gedicht und ebenfalls von der epischen oder erzählenden Art, wiewol die Handlung darinnen größtentheils Leiden ist.

Es hat einige Ähnlichkeit mit dem lezten Gesang der Ilias, wo die Klagen der Andromache, der Hecuba, und der Helena, und Hectors Leichenbegängniß vorkommen.

> Bodmer in the preface to his partial *Nibelungenlied* edition (1757), p. VIII.

Ueberhaupt giebt der Poet seinen vornehmsten Personen Empfindungen von Ehre, Großmuth, und Redlichkeit, die wir bey Homers Helden nicht in demselben offenbaren Lichte antreffen.

> Bodmer in the preface to his partial *Nibelungenlied* edition (1757), p. VIII.

Man siehet keinen Anschein, daß er jemals werde ganz gedrukt werden. Es ist in der That für den Ruhm des schwäbischen Zeitpunktes am besten gesorget, wenn man nicht alles, was noch in dem Staube verborgen liget, an den Tag hervorziehet, sondern in dem, was man uns giebt, eine reife und einsichtsvolle Wahl beobachtet. Das Ausnehmende in dieser alten Literatur ist eben nicht im Ueberflusse übrig.

> Bodmer in the preface to his partial *Nibelungenlied* edition (1757), p. X, about the two thirds of the text which he had cut.

Bodmers Verherrlichung des Stoffes und der Vergleich mit dem Maß aller Dinge, der Homerischen Ilias, sind als Ursprung der nationalen Auslegung des Nibelungenmythos zu sehen.

> Tobias Hermann Kehm in his book *Der Nibelungenmythos im Ersten Weltkrieg. Die Entstehung kontrafaktischer Narrationen und deren Wirkung auf das Geschichtsbewusstsein* (2015), p. 29.

Eh die aonischen Musen in Deutschlands hainen gewandelt,
Als Achilles noch nicht in deutschen gesängen gefochten,
Und Ulysses die freyer noch nicht im bettler betrogen,
Sangen die Eschilbache, von deutschen Musen begeistert,
Eigne gesänge, die frucht des selbst erfindenden geistes.
Einer von ihnen sang mit Mäonides tone die schwester,
Welcher die brüder den theueen [sic] gemahl erschlugen, die schwester
Wieder die brüder erschlug. Die zeit hat den nahmen getilget,

Aber sein lied gerettet, ich hab' es gehört, und ich will es
Lauter singen, es soll vom Rhein zur Ostsee ertönen.

> Bodmer's proem, which, in Homeric manner, he added to his partial translation of the *Nibelungenlied* entitled *Die Rache der Schwester* (1767).

Der Nibelungen Lied könnte die teutsche Ilias werden.

> The Swiss historian Johannes Müller in the second volume of his Swiss history, *Der Geschichten schweizerischer Eidgenossenschaft Anderes Buch* (1786), p. 121.

Der Akzent liegt auf dem Konjunktiv, denn Müller verlangte analog zur homerischen eine eigene Nibelungenphilologie [...].

> Otfrid Ehrismann (2002), p. 171, on the former quotation in a standard textbook about the epoch and the reception of the *Nibelungenlied*.

Voß soll sich sehr hart gegen dich bei der Rudolphi über dich ausgelassen haben, weil diese ihm erzahlte, auch du habest von den Nibelungen gesagt, sie konnten uns gewissermassen, waß den Griechen der Homer sein, er sagte unter andern, daß heiße einen Saustall einem Pallast vergleichen [...]

> Clemens Brentano in a letter to Achim von Arnim, written between 1 and 5 October 1805.

Von J. H. Voss wird berichtet, daß er das Nibelungenlied in seiner Schule zu Eurin im Auszuge lesen ließ.

> Hermann Leopold Köster in his *Geschichte der deutschen Jugendliteratur* (³1920), p. 233.

Schöpfer unsterblicher Namen, obgleich selbst namelos, Grab sey
    Erd' oder Ozean dir,
Erd' und Ozean halten dich nicht, dein gewaltiger Geist fuhr
    Auf zu der Halle des Lichts,
Deren goldene Pforte des tuscischen Dantes gedreyter
    Schlüssel eröfnet und schliesst;
Wo am Throne Homerus, Parthenias, Virgil, den Finger
    Uber die Lippe gelegt,
Majestätisch in Demut den spätern Machtton der Miltons
    Harfe entrauschet, behorcht:

Dir an der Seite sizt dort, der uns dich erklärte, der Sänger
  Noahs, noch selbst unerklärt;
Ja Ihm danken wir es, dass in Sivrit ein bessrer Achilleus
  Wieder vom Grabe erstand.
Zwar keiner Göttin Sohn, doch würdiger Halbgott zu heissen
  Als den dein Meister uns sang!
War nicht Homerus dein Meister? Die Funken homerischer Geister
  Wehn in des Nibelungs Nacht.
Lächelt ewig auf Andromaches Wange die Thräne?
  Weinet nicht Chremhild wie sie?

> Johann Heinrich Füssli's poem 'Der Dichter der Schwesterrache' on the anonymous poet of the *Nibelungenlied* (1800/1810), qtd. in Joachim Heinzle's anthology *Mythos Nibelungen* (2013), p. 201. 'The singer of Noah' ('der Sänger Noahs') refers to Bodmer, who had written an epic about the patriarch (*Noah, ein Heldengedicht* 1750/52).

In dem geflügelten Wohllaut der Sprache und des Versbaues, in den sich so lieblich an alle Dinge und ihre Eigenschaften anschmiegenden Benennungen, auch in der Ruhe und Besonnenheit, der Reinheit der epischen Form, ist Homer unerreichbar. Was aber Lebendigkeit und Gegenwart der Darstellung, dann die Größe der Leidenschaften, Charaktere, und der ganzen Handlung betrifft, darf sich das Lied der Nibelungen kühnlich mit der Ilias messen, ich würde sagen, es thut es ihr zuvor, wenn man es sich nicht zum Gesetze machen müßte, nie ein Meisterwerk auf Unkosten des andern zu loben.

> August Wilhelm Schlegel in his Berlin lectures on the *History of Romantic Literature* (*Geschichte der romantischen Litteratur*) 1802/03.

Fast hätte ich das beste Vergessen, Tieck hat mir seine trefliche Bearbeitung, und Ergänzung des Niebelungen Liedes, des einzigen uns wirklich angehörenden Epos vorgelesen, es erregt einen Eindruck uns selbst herrlicher und größer als Homer, und die ganze Zeit (dunkle) um Atila ist hell und klar, es hat bewiesen, daß es historisch Wahr ist, es ist sein größtes Verdienst, diese Wiederherstellung.

> Clemens Brentano in a letter to Friedrich Karl von Savigny, early March 1805.

Der wesentliche Vortheil also, den die Annahme unsers Vorschlages gewähren würde, das Lied der Nibelungen zu einem Hauptbuche der

Erziehung zu machen, es gründlich in den Schulen zu erklären und dem Gedächtnisse der Jugend einzuprägen, wäre der, den Geschichten unsers Volkes einen dichterischen Hintergrund zu geben, woran es ihnen bisher ganz und gar gefehlt hat. Von dieser Seite kann dieß Werk für uns eben das werden, was Homer den Griechen war.

> A. W. Schlegel 1812 in *Deutsches Museum*, p. 32.

Wie der einzelne Mensch so auch die Nation ruht auf dem Altvorhandenen, Ausländischen oft mehr als auf dem Eigenen, Ererbten und Selbstgeleisteten; aber nur in so fern ein Volk eigene Literatur hat, kann es urtheilen und versteht die vergangene wie die gleichzeitige Welt. [...] Der Deutsche war auf gutem Weg und wird ihn gleich wieder finden, sobald er das schädliche Bestreben aufgibt, die Nibelungen der Ilias gleichzustellen.

> Goethe 1817 in his periodical *Über Kunst und Altertum*, qtd. in Gunter E. Grimm, 'Goethe und das Nibelungenlied, Eine Dokumentation' (2006).

Haben wir Deutsche nicht unsern herrlichen Nibelungen durch solche Vergleichung den größten Schaden gethan?

> Goethe 1819 in his 'Noten und Abhandlungen' to his *West–östlicher Divan*, qtd. in Grimm (2006).

Und wie euch erst Homer gesungen
Erfreut ihr euch der Nibelungen

> Goethe in a fragment dating 1821, qtd. in Grimm (2006).

Das Klassische nenne ich das Gesunde, und das Romantische das Kranke. Und da sind die Nibelungen klassisch wie der Homer, denn beide sind gesund und tüchtig.

> Goethe 1821, in conversation with Johann Peter Eckermann, qtd. in Grimm (2006).

Ilias und *Odyssee* bleiben unterschöpflich ... An Folgen aus den *Nibelungen* fehlt es uns nicht, und ich denke daran, daß sie zu überbieten sind; denn meist werden die Heldengestalten des Mittelalters nur als travestierte Wesen des höhern griechischen Stils anzusehen sein.

> Goethe 1830, qtd. in Hartmut Fröschle, *Goethes Verhältnis zur Romantik* (2002), p. 477.

Die Jugend, aus sich selbst, nimmt keinen Antheil daran, wie an Homer. Und wer mir das widerspricht, der wird seine Erfahrung unter dem Bedenken zurücknehmen müssen, daß, wo ja die Nibelungen erklärt werden, es meist durch einen begeisterten Kenner geschieht, dessen Antheil und vielleicht geistvolle, gewiß aber liebevolle Behandlung mehr fesselt als die Sache selbst, während Homer das einzige Buch der Welt ist, dem in einem irgend sinnigen Knaben auch die Mishandlung des ärgsten Pedanten nur wenigen Schaden thut. Wenn man uns doch nicht mit dem schönen Gedanken einer Nationalerziehung ködern und fangen wollte! Eine Nation, die die Bibel und den Homer zu ihren Erziehungsbüchern gemacht hat, die sich am besten Mark der ganzen Menschheit nähren will, eine solche Nation kann einem solchen Werke, wie die Nibelungen, keinen so bevorzugenden Rang unter ihren Bildungs- und Unterrichtsmitteln gönnen; sie bleibt trotz ewigen Widersprüchen der Klüglinge auf dem betretenen Wege mit fester Ausdauer, während die Begeisterung für unsre alten Poesien von heute und gestern ist, und aus Zeiten die von einer Deutschthümelei befallen waren, über die wir mit kaltem Blute lachen.

In his *History of the Germans' National Literature* (*Geschichte der poetischen National-Literatur der Deutschen* 1835, here p. 272), Georg Gottfried Gervinus includes a digression, in which he argues against the idea of the 'German *Iliad*' and against the notion of reading the *Nibelungenlied* in lower grades in school.

Dem Knaben, dem werdenden Menschen, können die Helden der Nibelungen die achäischen des Homer nicht ersetzen. Die Strebsamkeit, das Feuer, das Vertrauen auf menschliche Kraft, von dem diese beseelt sind, kann allein Menschen von tüchtiger Art bilden, die Passivität dieser alten Germanen, die ihre heidnische Unruhe schon mit einer gewissen Schläfrigkeit vertauscht haben, kann uns nicht das Geschlecht schaffen, das den gegenwärtigen Zeiten gegenüber nothwendig ist.

Gervinus 1835, p. 273.

Wir fühlen uns schwerlich diesen Burgundern verwandter, als den Achäern des Homer, die uns doch noch Liebe zum Vaterlande lehren können, für das im ganzen Mittelalter nicht einmal der Name existirt. Wenn man vollends den poetischen Werth im vaterländischen Dünkel dem Homer entgegenzustellen kühn genug war, so muß man bedauern, daß so wenig

Kunstsinn unter uns herrscht, daß Aussprüche der Art nur eine Möglichkeit sind [...]

Gervinus 1835, p. 273.

Mit Recht sind Nibelungen und Kudrun in einem ähnlichen Verhältniss aufgefasst worden wie Ilias und Odyssee. Der großartige Hintergrund macht jene wie die Nibelungen gewaltiger und erschütternder; die Schicksale von ganzen Völkern werden mit dem Schwerte entschieden, ein Herrscherhaus, dem edle Helden angehören, geht vor unsern Augen dem Untergange entgegen. Aber auch die Sieger erfreuen sich des Glückes nicht; das Schicksal ist auch über sie hereingebrochen. Das Ganze athmet den Geist einer Tragödie, und mehr noch als in dem griechischen tritt in dem deutschen Epos dieser zum Tragischen sich gipfelnde Charakter hervor. Alles gewinnt dramatisches Leben: mit fieberhafter Spannung wird der Hörer durch alle Stufen des sicherschreitenden Verderbens geführt. 'Nach Freude Leid', ist der ernste Klang, der durch das ganze Nibelungenlied hindurchgeht [...]

Karl Bartsch in his edition of the *Kudrun* (1865), pp. xv–xvi.

Verdienen Nibelungenlied und Gudrun mit Recht die deutsche Ilias und Odysse genannt zu werden?

Hermann Kluge, *Themata zu deutschen Aufsätzen und Vorträgen, für höhere Unterrichtsanstalten* (^{2}1879), p. 29.

The [book] is an attempt to popularize for children the substance of the old Nibelungen Lied, the national poem of the Germans. An immense amount of ingenuity, learning, and research has been spent in determining the origin of this lay, which stands to the German race much as Homer stands to the Greeks and the legend of Arthur to us.

Review of Lydia Hands' *Golden Threads from an Ancient Loom*, 'Christmas Books', *The Times*, 16/12/1879.

Modern German critics agree in assigning a high literary value to the poem of Gu-drun [sic], and compare it not unfavorably with the Nibelungen Lied. Bartsch, the critic above named, says: "The general impression which the poem gives is one of greater beauty, though not always of equal grandeur with that of the Nibelungen; it is a worthy companion-piece. The two are justly compared, as are the Iliad and the Odyssey. In the Nibelungen as in the Iliad the fate of a whole people is decided by the sword, and the ruling house, consisting of noble heroes, meets destruction before our eyes; but the conquerors do not fully rejoice in their success. The whole breathes a tragic spirit, even more than the Greek epic. 'Nach Freude Leid' – 'after joy comes sorrow' – is the earnest tone throughout. [...]"

> This extract from Bartsch's introduction to his edition of *Kudrun* appeared in the first full English translation of that text: Mary Pickering Nichols, *Gudrun: A Medieval Epic* (1889), p. v.

It is truly wonderful, with what skill our simple untaught Poet deals with the marvellous; admitting it without reluctance or criticism, yet precisely in the degree and shape that will best avail him. Here, if in no other respect, we should say that he has a decided superiority to Homer himself. ... The Singer of the 'Nibelungen' is a far different person from Homer; far inferior both in culture and in genius. Nothing of the glowing imagery, of the fierce, bursting energy, of the mingled fire and gloom, that dwell in the old Greek, makes its appearance here. The German Singer is comparatively a simple nature; has never penetrated deep into life; never 'questioned Fate'; or struggled with fearful mysteries; of all which we find traces in Homer, still more in Shakespeare; but with meek, believing submission, has taken the Universe as he found it represented to him; and rejoices with a fine childlike gladness in the mere outward shows of things.

> Thomas Carlyle, *Westminster Review*, 1831

In conclusion, we must again say how strange it seems to us, that this Volsung Tale, which is in fact an unversified poem, should never before have been translated into English. For this is the Great Story of the North, which should be to all our race what the Tale of Troy was to the Greeks – to all our race first, and afterwards, when the change of the world has made our race nothing more than a name of what has been – a story too – then should it be to those that come after us no less than the Tale of Troy has been to us.

> William Morris and Eiríkr Magnússon in the preface to their book *Völsunga Saga: The Story of the Volsungs and Niblungs, with Certain Songs from the Elder Edda* (1870), p. xi.

My dear Boys and Girls,
> You are sure to like Sigurd, or Siegfried, by whichever name you choose to call him. He is the model of manliness. His wife, Gudrun,

or Kriemhild, you will pity and, for her sorrows, in pitying her you will forgive her for her cruel revenge. As to the whole story, you cannot help liking that if you are a true child of the North for, as William Morris has said, it is 'the Great Story of the North which should be to all our race what the Tale of Troy was to the Greeks,' and, as Thomas Carlyle said, 'it has meaning and charms for us.'

> From Thomas Cartwright's short preface to his children's book *Sigurd the Dragon Slayer: A Twice-Told Tale* (1907).

In the place they occupy in the national literature and in the relation which they bear to one another, the German *Nibelungenlied* and the *Gudrun* resemble the *Iliad* and the *Odyssey* of the Greeks. In the *Nibelungenlied* the tragic fate of Troy has its counterpart in the total extinction of the Burgundians, while in both the *Odyssey* and the *Gudrun* the accompaniment to battles and adventures is always the beat of the waves

> Margaret Armour, *Gudrun* (1928), p. v.

[...] es war sein Unglück, daß es erst zusammen mit der Wiederentdeckung Homers, Mitte des 18. Jahrhunderts, ins Bewußtsein der deutschen Kultur zurückkehrte. Dadurch wurde es von Anfang an als 'deutsche Ilias' festgelegt, und dieser zunächst plausibel erscheinende Vergleich war für das NL bald mörderisch, denn es handelt sich, obwohl beides Dichtungen von Weltrang sind, um zwei grundverschiedene Dinge [...]

> Franz Fühmann in the concept for a film adaptation of the *Nibelungenlied*, which he submitted in 1971 to the GDR film studio DEFA, qtd. in *Der Nibelunge Not* (1993), p. 151.

Illustration 8: Poster for 'Violent Victorian Medievalism'. Design by Katherine Beard, Linacre College, Oxford

MARY BOYLE
The Victorian *Nibelungenlied*

The essay brings two themes together of the reception of the *Nibelungenlied* which, *mutatis mutandis*, also apply to the adaptation of the Homeric poems in the Victorian era: the fascination with medieval violence and the difficulty in translating this for children.[1]

Violent Victorian Medievalism

> medievalism, *n.*
>
> 'the reception, interpretation or recreation of the European Middle Ages in post-medieval cultures', Louise D'Arcens, 2016[2]

A portcullis creaks. Dismembered corpses litter the snow. An unwashed man dismounts and looks on in terror. Just minutes into the first episode of *Game of Thrones* (HBO, 2011–19), the scene is set. This world, visually coded as medieval, is brutal. Such a trope crops up again and again in contemporary popular culture, often clearly taking a lead from HBO's era-defining series. Even puppets were beheaded in the teaser for *The Green Knight* (A24, 2021), while trailers for other medievalist films and television programmes over the past decade repeatedly emphasise barbarity and bloodshed: *Vikings* (History, 2013–), *The Last Kingdom* (BBC, Netflix, 2015–), *Outlaw King* (Netflix, 2018). One of the latest iterations is called, simply, *Medieval* (WOG FILM s.r.o., 2022). But despite defending the violence

---

[1] The first essay was published as 'Violent Medievalism, Violent Victorians' as part of the volume 'Violent Victorian Medievalism', ed. by Mary Boyle, Oxford 2022, the second as 'Translating Medieval Violence: What's Acceptable for Children?' by Mary Boyle on the Queen's Translation Exchange blog in 2021, and then in the catalogue of the 'Violent Victorian Medievalism' exhibition. Reissued with permission.

[2] Louise D'Arcens, 'Introduction: Medievalism: scope and complexity', in *The Cambridge Companion to Medievalism* (Cambridge, 2016), pp. 1–13.

in *A Song of Ice and Fire / Game of Thrones* by saying, 'It's not the Disneyland Middle Ages', George R.R. Martin did not rip the Band-Aid off a shared vision of a utopian Middle Ages to reveal historically accurate and hitherto unexplored gore. In truth, the idea that 'medieval' is a synonym for violent, even when not explicitly articulated, runs through later responses to the period, from the cerebral to the popular.

Enter the Victorians. A fascination with the Middle Ages shaped public life in the nineteenth century – and in exchange, it reshaped the Middle Ages into a form still dominant today. Englishness became inextricably connected with a reimagined medieval past expressed through art, architecture, and literature. English traits and values were traced to a Golden Age of chivalry, and a national character was anchored in a heroic so-called Germanic past (also described as Anglo-Saxon, Northern, or Teutonic). The longevity of this tradition is evident in the 2021 St George's Day Google Doodle.[3] But chivalry and heroism necessarily exist within a martial context, and violence already permeated the geopolitics, literature, and culture of Britain's 'imperial century'. Abroad, Britain added 400 million people and 10 million square miles to its Empire, at the cost of countless lives.[4] At home, cheap and garishly illustrated penny dreadfuls sold in huge numbers thanks to rising literacy rates and an increased appetite for entertainment.[5] This taste for melodrama gave rise to the sensation novel which – supposedly – had a more respectable audience. It catered, though, to an equivalent taste for bloodshed.[6] Medieval or medieval-adjacent literature offered another respectable vehicle for violence. In the 1830s, Thomas Carlyle published an essay

---

[3] '23 April 2021: St. George's Day 2021', *Google*, 2021.
[4] Timothy Parsons, *The British Imperial Century, 1815-1914: A World History Perspective* (Lanham, Boulder, New York, Toronto, and Oxford, 1999), p. 3.
[5] For more information on the penny dreadful, see Judith Flanders, 'Victorian Penny Dreadfuls', brewminate, 2019.
[6] For more information on sensation novels, see Matthew Sweet, *Inventing the Victorians* (2001).

drawing the nation's attention to a medieval epic, 'belong[ing] especially to us English *Teutones*'.[7] This was the *Nibelungenlied*, a story of love, betrayal, vengeance, and hopeless heroism. It had already been decreed a potential 'German *Iliad*' – and, like the *Iliad*, its body count was vast.[8] With its frequent scenes of graphic violence and potential for ethnonationalist identity construction, the narrative incorporated various national pursuits for the Victorians. They revelled in it, as did the Edwardians – right up to the First World War.

The *Nibelungenlied*

> Uns ist in alten mæren wunders vil geseit
> von helden lobebæren, von grôzer arebeit,
> von fröuden, hôchgeziten, von weinen und von klagen,
> von küener recken strîten muget ir nu wunder hœren sagen
> *The Nibelungenlied*, stanza 1
>
> In ancient tales, we are told much of wonder: of praiseworthy heroes, of great toil, of joys, festivals, of tears and laments, and of brave warriors battling, now you may hear wonders told.

The *Nibelungenlied* is the most famous German version of a collection of heroic legends known also in various Scandinavian incarnations. It tells of the dragon-slaying hero Siegfried and his arrival in Burgundy, where he hopes to woo the famously beautiful Princess Kriemhild. Various obstacles – or opportunities to prove himself – present themselves. He fights off invading Danes and Saxons and, through dishonest means, helps Kriemhild's brother Gunther win the hand of the warrior queen, Brünhild, after which Siegfried and Kriemhild are also married. Years later, while Siegfried and Kriemhild are visiting Burgundy, tensions erupt, and Gunther conspires with his vassal, Hagen, to have Siegfried murdered. Hagen stabs him in the back while they are hunting in the forest, and leaves his body

---

[7] Thomas Carlyle, 'Das Nibelungen Lied, übersetzt von Karl Simrock (The "Nibelungen Lied", translated by Karl Simrock.) 2 Vols. 12mo. Berlin. 1827.', *Westminster Review*, 15/29 (1831), p. 4. See the essay by Philip Flacke in this volume.

[8] Johannes von Müller, *Der Geschichten schweizerischer Eidgenossenschaft. Anderes Buch. Von dem Aufblühen der ewigen Bünde* (Leipzig, 1786), II, p. 121.

outside Kriemhild's door. Hagen then steals her treasure hoard, a gift from Siegfried, and sinks it in the Rhine, ostensibly to prevent her from using it to gain allies in pursuit of revenge.

Years pass, and Kriemhild accepts a marriage proposal from Etzel, King of the Huns, hoping to find an opportunity to avenge Siegfried. She invites the Burgundians to visit her and engineers an outbreak of violence. Ultimately, almost nobody is left alive, and Gunther and Hagen, the last surviving Burgundians, are brought before her. She orders her brother to be killed and brings his head to Hagen, before decapitating Hagen with Siegfried's sword. A bystander, outraged that this fearsome warrior has been killed by a woman, strikes Kriemhild down himself, and the poet concludes:

> Ine kan iu niht bescheiden, waz sider dâ geschach,
> wan ritter und vrouwen weinen man dá sach,
> dar zuo die edeln knehte, ir lieben friunde tôt.
> dâ hât daz mære ein ende. diz ist der Nibelunge nôt.
> *The Nibelungenlied*, stanza 2376
>
> I cannot tell you what happened there later, only that knights and ladies were seen weeping, noble squires too, their dear friends dead. Here the story has an end: this is the Nibelungs' distress.

After Carlyle's essay, anglophone adaptations began to appear, initially as a trickle and then, following the first performances of Richard Wagner's *Ring des Nibelungen*, as a flood. Writers often adapted not only the *Nibelungenlied* itself, but combined it with the other Scandinavian and German narratives associated with its characters, and introduced elements from their own imaginations – just as Wagner had done. The resulting adaptations were aimed at all age groups and educational levels, and many were eye-catchingly illustrated. While the slightest allusion to sex was usually avoided in Victorian and Edwardian adaptations (as opposed to translations) of this material, gruesome violence tended to make it through, including in those versions aimed at children. Indeed, it often appeared in picture form: a woman brandishes the decapitated head of her brother; a man is stabbed in the back while drinking from a spring; a knight faces up to a fearsome dragon. Some illustrators stopped short of depicting the violence itself, but were happy to depict the moments immediately before or after: the spear poised to leave a hand and enter a back; piles of corpses. This predilection for carnage has echoes of modern children's educational entertainment like *Horrible Histories* (CBBC, 2009–2020, based on Terry Deary's book series, 1993-2013), which was marketed as 'history with the nasty bits left in', but it was also par for the course in the long nineteenth century (1789–1914), and was certainly not limited to the items on display in this exhibition. Lucy H. Fleming's contribution to the 2022 catalogue on children's adaptations of Chaucer, for example, casts light on another tradition of medievalist violence in the nineteenth century.

The *Nibelungenlied*, along with its associated material, however, was so widely reinterpreted in the long nineteenth century, and so emblematic for notions of a so-called Germanic identity, that it provides a useful prism through which to demonstrate the wider implications of violent Victorian (and Edwardian) medievalism.[9] Children's literature of this period routinely matched a reticence about sex with scenes of extreme violence, often while simultaneously smuggling in an educational message. In adaptations of the *Nibelungenlied* and other related legends, that message was unequivocal, both for children and for adults: this narrative is your cultural inheritance. We can thus see the connection forged between (ethno-)nationalist nostalgia and a violence that can often be parsed as heroic or fantastical, thus neutering potential charges of sensationalism. It is a clear forerunner of twentieth- and twenty-first-century children's medievalism, as well as mapping on to more recent trends in violent medievalism and popular culture.

---

[9] Because such tendencies continue beyond the strict boundaries of the Victorian era, as far as the outbreak of the First World War, the original exhibition included items published up to twelve years after Victoria's death.

Epic Adaptations for Children

Illustration 9: 'The maiden hurled her spear'
MacGregor 1908 (section 4), facing p. 76. Playmobil figure of a Viking.
Photograph: Henrike Lähnemann

Knights and dragons are such a fixture of children's literature that they seem to find their way into the least medieval settings imaginable. Not only is there even a *Postman Pat* episode on the topic but, since I started writing this, I've discovered that there are two, 'Postman Pat and the Greendale Knights' (2007) and 'Postman Pat and the King's Armour' (2017). But have you ever stopped to think about how strange this is? Dragons are bloodthirsty monsters, while the business of knights is, well, violence. It might be characterised as violence in the service of their country, or to protect damsels in distress, but it's violence nonetheless. The purpose of those swords isn't simply to shine, but to kill – or at the very least to threaten to kill. And yet we think of these characters as not just child-friendly, but obvious material for children's stories. Why?

Fitting knights and their world into children's literature isn't a new idea, but goes back well over a hundred years, to Victorian and Edwardian children's authors who made use of medieval texts in their search for new material for young audiences. Drawing on the past is never politically neutral, and it certainly wasn't for these writers, who were getting involved in a contemporary passion for the Middle Ages which was so influential that many of the things we think of today as medieval are actually products of the nineteenth century.[10] So why wasn't this politically neutral? Countless words have been written about this, but to cut a long story short and then simplify it, there was a desire to identify the beginnings of English culture and democracy in a pre-Norman-Conquest past which was shared with other supposedly 'Germanic' (itself a complicated and loaded term) regions like Germany and Scandinavia. Given this background, maybe it's not surprising that writers at the time decided that the *Nibelungenlied* would make a perfect children's book. After all, it featured not only those knights and dragons, but also other fairy-tale staples like kings, queens, princes, princesses, treasure, prophecies, and battles.

---

[10] For more on this, see my blogpost 'The Medievalism Onion: Layers of Interpretation', *TORCH*, 2020 [accessed 11 May 2024].

Unfortunately, the *Nibelungenlied* also has pretty non-child-friendly features: sex and sexual violence; betrayal and (mass) murder; the decapitation of a child; burning people alive; drinking blood from corpses; the parading of the decapitated head of one prisoner in front of another; the beheading of an unarmed man; and – to close proceedings – the brutal killing of a woman. Basically, the knights behave like the warriors they are – but it's worth pointing out that, generally speaking, the violence itself wasn't exactly a problem for our writers. The real issue was that much of the violence is directed (and partly carried out) by a woman, our main character, Kriemhild.

Turning the *Nibelungenlied* into a children's story obviously wasn't going to be just a matter of translating it from Middle High German into English and putting it in the hands of young Victorians. The mostly fairy-tale-like first half of the narrative was quite easily adapted for children, but the second part presented many more problems because the plot basically follows Kriemhild's violent quest for revenge. Now admittedly, it could have been worse – the Scandinavian material features the female protagonist killing her children, baking them into pies, and serving them to their father. At least Kriemhild's limit was putting her son in a situation which she knew would lead to his death in order to further her revenge plot. One common solution was to adapt only the first part, perhaps summarising the revenge plot in a few sentences. These adaptations would usually bring in some Scandinavian material, which had the advantage over the German version that the fight with the dragon didn't take place 'offscreen'. This particular violence only involves a man and a monster, so it could appear in its full gory detail, including Siegfried's post-fight bath in the dragon's blood. But there were some writers who decided that they were just going to go for it and adapt the whole thing. Let's take a look at two of them.

First up, Lydia Hands, author of *Golden Threads from an Ancient Loom*, subtitled *Das Nibelungenlied, adapted to the use of young readers*. She was ahead of the curve by publishing in 1880 – most English-language children's adaptations of the *Nibelungenlied* came along after the English premiere of Wagner's *Ring* cycle in 1882 drew attention to the material. Hands deals with the difficulty of translating Kriemhild's violence by finding an explanation which would make (legal) sense to her audience: Kriemhild was mad with grief at the death of her child. You're probably thinking that this is a bit rich of Kriemhild, since this is entirely her own fault. So Hands simply neglects to translate that part of the text. In her version, the boy's death comes as a terrible shock, causing Kriemhild to faint in horror. When she wakes up, 'a frenzy, as of madness, possessed Criemhild; her enemy should not escape, even though her own life should be the penalty'. Then she orders the hall to be burned down with hundreds of men inside. It's the death of her son that triggers Kriemhild's madness, and her madness which triggers her indiscriminate violence. Insanity was a routine defence in nineteenth-century law courts, and it means that Hands can keep all the violence – and she *really* does – without undermining contemporary expectations of women. It doesn't excuse Kriemhild, and she doesn't get a happy ending, just a marginally less violent death, but it relieves her of her moral responsibility and any knock-on consequences for society.

This wasn't enough for Gertrude Schottenfels in *Stories of the Nibelungen for Young People* in 1905. There's no violent death for Kriemhild's son, and Kriemhild herself is kept at some distance from the violence. Eventually, Hagen and Gunther are brought to her by a knight, who makes her give 'her word of honor that he, and he alone, should be permitted to put them to death'. So really, when Kriemhild orders them to be beheaded 'according to the custom of these olden times', she's just following a knight's suggestion. This Kriemhild is allowed to live, and the closest we get to a condemnation is being told that she was 'once gentle and beautiful', implying that she no longer is. But she's neither dead nor disgraced, and the spectacular body count isn't attributed to her. – Maybe this is as close as we get to an answer to my starting question. Compared to the other violence in the *Nibelungenlied*, knights' (and dragons') violence isn't considered a big deal. As long as you can translate away the unacceptable violence, you can keep the rest – no matter how extreme.

Illustration 10: Franz Fühmann's film script (section 3) in the stacks of the Taylorian. Photograph: Philip Flacke

Timothy Powell
The *Nibelungenlied* from National Socialist Epic to Socialist National Epic

> Es gilt heute, das NL [*Nibelungenlied*] als Erbe überhaupt in Besitz zu nehmen. Dabei könnte ein Film eine hervorragende Rolle spielen. Es wäre ein Beitrag, den nur die sozialistische Nationalkultur leisten kann. (Franz Fühmann)[1]
>
> Today's task is to take ownership of the *Nibelungenlied* as heritage. A film could play an outstanding role in this. This would be a contribution only a socialist national culture can make.

How to transform a National Socialist epic into a socialist national epic? In his screenplay *Der Nibelunge Not* (1973), Franz Fühmann (1922–84) boldly attempts to rehabilitate the *Nibelungenlied* for the national canon of the German Democratic Republic after two centuries of misinterpretation and misuse. Fühmann's screenplay was only published posthumously in the GDR in 1987, and remains both unfilmed and notably under-researched in comparison to other aspects of his writing, much of which has itself fallen into obscurity as a result of the large-scale displacement of GDR literature from the post-reunification canon. However, *Der Nibelunge Not* deserves much more attention in critical debates surrounding the reception of classical and medieval epic and the emergence of the concept of a German 'national epic'. In this screenplay, Fühmann radically rejects Enlightenment traditions of reception of the *Nibelungenlied* as 'the German *Iliad*' – and their culmination under National Socialism – in order to rehabilitate the epic as an indispensable element of the 'socialist national culture' of the German Democratic Republic.

---

[1] Fühmann, Franz, 'Szenarium für einen Spielfilm "Das Nibelungenlied"', in Franz Fühmann, *Der Nibelunge Not. Szenarium für einen Spielfilm*, ed. Peter Göhler (Berlin: Aufbau Taschenbuch Verlag, 1993), p. 153 (= *SfeS*). This essay is an adapted extract from a dissertation submitted for the degree of Master of Studies in Modern Languages at the University of Oxford in Trinity Term 2023.

Fühmann's bold claim in the introductory quotation from *Szenarium für einen Spielfilm* – his 1971 film proposal to the DEFA – that the *Nibelungenlied* needed to be reclaimed 'als Erbe überhaupt' (*SfeS*, p. 153) highlights how little engagement with the epic had occurred during the first twenty years of cultural production in the GDR. Just ten versions of the *Nibelungenlied* (and the related Siegfried matter) were produced in the GDR between 1956 and 1971.[2] Four only indirectly drew on the epic via early modern *Volksbücher* – popular versions of highlights from its fairytale and adventure story elements. Three were modern German editions and translations of the epic, including one licensed West German edition. Just three literary texts directly engaged with the *Nibelungenlied* to creatively draw it into GDR national cultural heritage, two of which were Fühmann's own creations – the poem 'Der Nibelunge Not' (1957) and a prose retelling of the epic, *Das Nibelungenlied* (1971). The epic had also largely been relegated from the sphere of national cultural heritage to children's literature and literature for political interest groups. Five of the ten versions were printed by publishers of books for children and young people. What is more, the first ever GDR edition and translation appeared in 1957 with Verlag der Nation – the publisher of the *Nationaldemokratische Partei Deutschlands*, a bloc party for former National Socialists and *Wehrmacht* officers – of which, incidentally, Fühmann had himself been a member between 1950 and 1972. The only adaptations published by more literary publishers were Fühmann's own poem (Aufbau, 1957), two Modern German editions and translations (Reclam, 1961 and Dieterich, 1964), and a Volksbuch edition (Insel, 1969).[3] The scarcity and obscurity of GDR interpretations of the epic before Fühmann's screenplay thus also vindicate his claim that it urgently needed to be more fully integrated into the national cultural heritage of the GDR of the early 1970s.

---

[2] Grosse, Siegfried and Ursula Rautenberg, *Die Rezeption mittelalterlicher deutscher Dichtung: Eine Bibliographie ihrer Übersetzungen und Bearbeitungen seit der Mitte des 18. Jahrhunderts* (Tübingen: Max Niemeyer Verlag, 1989), pp. 166-230.

[3] See Hueting, Gail A., 'Book Publishing in the German Democratic Republic', *The Library Quarterly: Information, Community, Policy*, Vol. 52, Nr. 3 (July 1982), pp. 240-59, for more detail on the GDR publishing industry.

Fühmann's sense of urgency to do so reflects wider contemporary concerns surrounding the reappraisal of pre-modern literature and culture and their integration into the national literary and cultural heritage of the GDR against the backdrop of the *Erbediskussion* – an ongoing academic and political debate about the composition and role of national heritage in the GDR. An important example of these emerging reflections in politics is the hardline SED and Kulturbund functionary Hans Koch's (1927-86) article 'Kulturbund und kulturelles Erbe', published in the Kulturbund weekly *Der Sonntag* on 25 May 1975. Koch attempts to make sense of the growing gulf between the rapidly expanding official definition of GDR national heritage and the significantly less rapidly expanding engagement with the often more obscure figures, artefacts and events that had recently been incorporated into it. Koch proposes that this lack of practical engagement is down to a lack of surviving information about the 'wealth of dialectical relationships' between factors such as the objective and subjective reality of historical figures, creators of artefacts and instigators of events, and their status within their 'class', society and wider humanity. He also warns that individual citizens' engagement with GDR national cultural heritage was being weakened by increasingly theoretical and representative official approaches to it. He is concerned that this would weaken ordinary people's ability to engage with it on a practical, everyday level to identify the knowledge and skills that a figure, cultural artefact or event revealed to be essential for individual and collective socialist life and to apply this to their own lives in the present.[4]

Finally, Koch acknowledges that the rapidly expanding definition of cultural heritage increasingly poses the question, 'Wie halten wir es mit der Reaktion?' – the *Gretchenfrage* of GDR cultural heritage – enquiring whether 'reactionary culture' could ever be considered part of 'socialist culture'. Taking the legend of Frederick Barbarossa, he highlights the differences between 'the historical core' and 'the clouds of nationalistic and militaristic stuffiness' surrounding it,

---

[4] Koch, Hans, 'Was, wäre zu fragen, ist unser Erbe?', Peter Lübbe (ed.), *Dokumente zur Kunst-, Literatur- und Kulturpolitik der SED, Band 3: 1975-1980* (Stuttgart: Seewald-Verlag, 1984), pp. 40-41 and 43. All following quotations Koch p. 44.

stressing that much formerly fascist cultural heritage could be integrated into socialist cultural heritage if it underwent 'a great intellectual cleansing'. Explicitly praising Fühmann's 1971 prose retelling of the *Nibelungenlied* as a model of socialist engagement with medieval literature which was once considered 'reactionary', he warns that reluctance to engage with such literary heritage in the GDR risked creating a cultural vacuum which, if not filled by 'progressive' reinterpretations of these texts, would be exploited by the West to openly continue nationalistic and militaristic misuse of them. Concluding that it is impossible to simply write 'the reaction and its further-reaching legacies' out of the canon, he argues that it is imperative for GDR cultural creators to overcome the 'cultural values of hatred and contempt' associated with such works during National Socialism and thereby reclaim these writings for the GDR canon.

Indeed, in contrast to the mere eleven GDR versions of the *Nibelungenlied* and the Siegfried subject matter, a whole 84 versions were produced by the so-called 'reactionary' cultural creators of West Germany before 1973.[5] This total includes 30 children's books and fairytales, 15 editions and translations, 14 narrative or epic retellings, 12 satirical or humorous takes, seven plays, four poems, and two editions of *Volksbuch* versions of the epic – not to mention two film adaptations by Artur Brauner (1966/67) and Adrian Hoven (1970). Although paper shortages and censorship would have been partly responsible for significantly fewer GDR versions of the *Nibelungenlied* having been produced, these factors alone cannot account for this enormous disparity between GDR and FRG editions of the subject matter. Grosse and Rautenberg's bibliography shows that West German writers and cultural figures had begun to re-engage with the *Nibelungenlied* as part of their literary heritage almost a decade earlier than their East German counterparts. They had also engaged with the epic in a more diverse range of genres, including drama, film and parody. Furthermore, they had republished ten earlier re-workings of the epic from 1827 to 1940 in no fewer than sixteen editions, re-

---

[5] This and the following after Grosse / Rautenberg (1989) 166-230.

covering and beginning to engage with editions of the *Nibelungenlied* published prior to the epic's misuse in post-Stalingrad National Socialist 'total war' propaganda which had rendered it culturally unacceptable for a time (see *SfeS*, p. 153), whereas not a single earlier edition had been republished in the GDR.

To overcome such historical baggage resulting from both historical misuse of German cultural heritage and what was perceived as its continuing misuse by Western 'reactionary forces', some East German academics developed new and innovative frameworks for reinterpreting and reclaiming literary texts and other artefacts that were considered important to pre-National Socialist cultural heritage. One contemporary approach which was particularly pertinent to works of medieval literature — especially the *Nibelungenlied* — was proposed by Wolfgang Spiewok (1929-99), Professor of Medieval German in Greifswald, in 1974. From reading Fühmann's own 1971 prose rendering of the *Nibelungenlied* through the lens of contemporary re-evaluations of Vladimir Lenin's cultural theory, Spiewok developed a 'socialist' approach to rehabilitating medieval texts. Spiewok's strategy begins with attaining 'the most historically objective assessment which opens up their true content', which, according to Marxist-Leninist sociology, was only available to the 'proletariat' as the final historical class freed from the concerns of previously dominant socio-economic groups.[6] Spiewok suggests that viewing medieval literature from this proletarian standpoint would enable it to undergo processes of 'party assessment' (*parteiliche Wertung*) which draw out its potential to contribute to the development of socialist individuals and society. Ultimately, Spiewok suggests that attaining a synthesis of this dialectic of objective and partisan interpretation of medieval texts would enable the reader to identify aspects of the text that promoted the 'socialist individual's' intellectual, emotional, moral and ideological development within society, and thus to fulfil the key criteria for admission into the new, 'socialist' national literature of the GDR.

---

[6] This and the following from Spiewok, Wolfgang, 'Zur Erbediskussion aus der Sicht der Mittelalterforschung', *Weimarer Beiträge*, Vol. 20 Nr. 1 (1974), p. 89.

Fühmann's screenplay begins transforming the *Nibelungenlied* into a socialist national epic by separating its subject matter from previous ideological (mis-)appropriations to arrive at the 'most historically objective' interpretation of the epic, qualifying it for recognition as GDR cultural heritage. He begins this process by rejecting the long-established concept of the epic as 'deutsche *Ilias*' (*SfeS*, p. 151), which he ascribes to the historical accident of its rediscovery at the same time as that of classical Homeric poetry in the eighteenth century. He claims that the failure to distinguish between the fundamentally different structures of Homeric and medieval society in the two epics led to Siegfried being misunderstood and misrepresented as a heroic central character *par excellence* (*SfeS*, p. 151), leading to all subsequent interpretations of the epic until National Socialism being skewed towards what he terms 'the reactionary' (*SfeS*, p. 151). To explore how Fühmann counters these 'reactionary' interpretations of the *Nibelungenlied*, Peter Göhler's observation that he presents Siegfried as creating great chaos as a foreign object in the feudal society of his adaptation[7] should be taken further to highlight how Fühmann consistently shows how this disruptive behaviour marks Siegfried out as an 'anachronistisch angelegte Figur' and 'Träger eines nicht-mehr-möglichen Verhaltens' (*SfeS*, p. 151), whose values (idealised by National Socialism) are impossible in modern society.

This notion is symbolically impressed upon the viewer from the beginning through the stage directions describing Siegfried's first appearance on screen: 'Plötzlich sprengt querfeldein eine Schar Reiter der Spitze der Heersäule zu.' (*DNN*, p. 31).[8] Here, Fühmann evokes the highly disruptive nature of Siegfried's character from his very first sudden and unexpected appearance in the world of the epic. In the *Szenarium*, Fühmann reveals how Siegfried cannot sustain his existence in the world of the epic after so violently bursting into it because he thinks in pre-feudal, individualistic categories of 'Abenteuer, Kampf, Jagd, Krieg, Landnahme, Liebe' instead of the more 'feudal',

---

[7] Göhler, Peter, 'Nachwort', *SfeS*, pp. 169–70; cf. also Göhler, Peter, 'Fühmanns Filmentwurf *Der Nibelunge Not*', Paul Alfred Kleinert (ed.), *Filmwelten Franz Fühmanns* (Berlin and Leipzig: Engelsdorfer Verlag, 2022), pp. 77–88, here p. 84.

[8] Franz Fühmann, *Der Nibelunge Not* (= *DNN*) in *SfeS*.

collectivist 'Staatsdenken' (*DNN*, p. 155) which dictates the thinking of all other characters in this world. For instance, Siegfried's conspicuous absence from the meeting of the royal council (*DNN*, pp. 34-36), despite his prominent role in the preceding and subsequent victory celebration scenes, emphasises how he displays no concept of thinking in the interests of the national and international collective, instead consistently thinking in his own interest. A particularly striking example occurs at the end of the first victory ceremony (*DNN*, pp. 32-34). When Gernot and Hagen make the captured kings of Saxony and Denmark kneel in submission before the Burgundian kings, Siegfried reveals that he simply released the king of the Goths because he grew tired of the latter's very bad grace in defeat. Gunther's exasperated comment that Siegfried's prisoner 'war das Haupt des Feindbunds. Nun, da er entkommen ist, wird er es wieder sein!' leads the latter to respond in an even more offhand manner than previously, 'Dann haun wir sie eben nochmals zusammen!' (*DNN*, p. 34).

This response reveals that, instead of thinking in 'feudal' categories of securing the interests of the collective of the state by defeating its enemies and securing peace with other states using astute strategic alliances, he still thinks in pre-feudal terms by seeing these enemies merely as personal adversaries to be crushed using brute force. By describing the way he expresses them as offhand, Fühmann suggests that these categories of Siegfried's thinking are wholly inadequate for the requirements of life in a complex modern society, dissuading the viewer from emulating them. This is compounded by Fühmann's use of the colloquial contracted form 'zusammenhaun' in Siegfried's comment, which is of a much lower register than that typically associated with courtly speech, highlighting at linguistic level how crude and outdated these militaristic ideals (reminiscent of National Socialist thinking) are in the modern world.

Siegfried's archaic status is most aptly reflected by Gere's comment that 'Er zog in Burgund ein wie irgendeiner der Urzeitrecken, von denen die Spielleute auf die Märkte singen!' (*DNN*, p. 35). This reflects traces of more archaic oral traditions associated with Siegfried that recur throughout the courtly poetic structure of the *Nibelungenlied*, such as Hagen's account of Siegfried's battle with the dragon, suggesting the potentially apocryphal nature of his exploits. Here, the simile describing Siegfried's entry into Burgundy underlines how outdated the frameworks which govern his behaviour are by associating them with an undefined, primal period which is so pre-historical as to be extra-historical. The other highly archaic term, 'Recke', in this compound noun also reinforces just how out-of-place Siegfried is by echoing the different linguistic levels of the *Nibelungenlied* which distinguish characters associated with historic Germanic heroic ideals from those associated with contemporary ideals of French courtly culture. The most ancient connotations of this word, associating Siegfried with the giants of ancient Germanic legend, denote him as a grotesque character whose attitudes and behaviour sharply contrast with those expected of a character in his position in medieval society. The term's further Old High German connotations of a 'hero driven out of his homeland'[9] also emphasise how Siegfried very clearly belongs to a different geographical and temporal homeland to the world of the screenplay. In addition to diminishing Siegfried's esteem in the eyes of the viewer by revealing Gere's highly dismissive attitude towards him, Fühmann's use of the indefinite pronoun 'irgendeiner' to qualify this compound noun reinforces the sense of defamiliarisation that he attaches to Siegfried throughout the screenplay. In these episodes, Fühmann therefore separates the epic from eighteenth-century German nationalist interpretations of it by differentiating between the social frameworks that govern the behaviour of pre-feudal and feudal characters, highlighting how Siegfried's 'reactionary', individualistic values and attitudes are unsustainable in modern societies much more oriented towards the needs and values of collectives of class, nation and the world at large.

---

[9] *Deutsches Wörterbuch von Jacob Grimm und Wilhelm Grimm* (= *DWB*), digitalisierte Fassung im Wörterbuchnetz des Trier Center for Digital Humanities, Version 01/23, vol. 14 (1887), 'recke, m.', www.woerterbuchnetz.de/DWB/recke.

Throughout the screenplay, Fühmann starkly contrasts the militaristic and inhumane qualities that he associates with 'pre-feudal' characters such as Siegfried with the more 'feudal' layers of the epic that he interprets as moving closer to the ideals of 'socialist culture' of the East German nation. This was defined by the 1968 GDR constitution as rooted in peace, humanism and international co-operation and actively opposing 'imperialist un-culture' rooted in warfare, cruelty and rivalrous nationalism.[10] An example of how Fühmann reinterprets the *Nibelungenlied* as a literary text that works against the glorification of violence to promote peace can be seen when the crowd falls silent after Gunther's angry retort to Siegfried that Burgundy's power was not built on daring and boldness, adding emphasis to his critique of Siegfried's militarism. In response to this silence, Gunther stands together with the defeated kings and proclaims that 'Versöhnung ist der Wille Burgunds!' and 'ruft ins Volk: Versöhnung! Frieden!', which the people jubilantly acclaim (*DNN*, p. 34). Fühmann's contrast between Siegfried's boldness and Gunther's irenic disposition reveals his rejection of Siegfried's warlike ideals in favour of new ideals of reconciliation and peace that look ahead to ideals of socialist internationalism, with which Fühmann encourages the audience to identify through the final stage direction in this scene highlighting the acclaim that this action receives from the ordinary people assembled there.

Fühmann also seeks to rehabilitate the *Nibelungenlied* by suggesting how it promotes Marxist ideals of 'socialist humanism', the essence of which is defined by Michael Kinne and Birgit Strube-Edelmann as 'elimination of all exploitation and oppression of the human being' which would be 'fully realised' 'in socialist and communist society'.[11] These humanist ideals of non-exploitation and non-oppression that Fühmann presents in *Der Nibelunge Not* can be observed in Fühmann's presentation of the Burgundian kings' respect for the human

---

[10] *Verfassung der Deutschen Demokratischen Republik vom 9. April 1968*, Artikel 18, https://www.verfassungen.de/ddr/verf68-i.htm.

[11] Kinne, Michael and Strube-Edelmann, Birgit, 'Sozialistischer Humanismus', in: Michael Kinne, Birgit Strube-Edelmann (edd.), *Kleines Wörterbuch des DDR-Wortschatzes* (Düsseldorf: Pädagogischer Verlag, 2nd edn. 1981), p. 185.

dignity of their captured Saxon and Danish counterparts. Before the defeated kings appear, two wounded knights from each army are brought on in 'zwei gepolsterten Wagen', which are 'ehrenvoll links und rechts neben den Thronen aufgestellt' (both *DNN*, p. 32). Here, Fühmann presents the Burgundians' dignified treatment of these wounded prisoners of war as a 'feudal' ancestor of these ideals of socialist humanism. Instead of being treated like objects and spoils of war, they are treated with the decency that human beings deserve, transported in comfort and treated with the same dignity afforded to the victors by remaining directly beside their thrones throughout the scene. This is reinforced by Fühmann's stage directions associated with the homage paid by the defeated king of Denmark, which stress that the scenes are to take place 'mit der höchsten Würde und keinesfalls mit Brutalität oder mit kleinlicher Schikane und Kränkung gegenüber den Gefangenen' (*DNN*, p. 33). This highly humane and dignified treatment of prisoners starkly contrasts with Siegfried's shockingly gratuitous violence against the defeated Wild Man: 'Siegfried lifts the wild man up high and smashes him onto the floorboards. The wild man's ribs shatter; blood gushes from his nose. Siegfried laughs as he places his foot on his neck' (*DNN*, p. 38), further discrediting Siegfried and the 'cultural values of hatred and contempt' associated with him by showing just how far removed the ideals he embodies are from those of the 'socialist' values of human dignity on which the GDR professed to be founded.

In addition, Fühmann clearly distances the *Nibelungenlied* from National Socialist misappropriations of it, which he suggests largely proceed from Enlightenment misinterpretations of Siegfried combined with *Gründerzeit* reworkings of it as a foundational epic for the new German Empire praising the ancient 'Germanic' values on which this new nation-state and society were purportedly founded. Werner Wunderlich's observation that Fühmann's screenplay, like his eponymous poem, is 'concerned with coming to terms with the Third Reich and the purposes to which it used the epic'[12] should be

---

[12] Wunderlich, Werner, 'Fühmann, Franz', in: Francis G. Gentry, Winder McConnell, Ulrich Müller, Werner Wunderlich (edd.), *The Nibelungen Tradition: An Encyclopedia* (New York/London: Routledge, 2002), p. 239.

taken further to investigate how Fühmann's screenplay actively works against the lingering influence of National Socialist appropriation of the epic. For instance, Fühmann's screenplay expressly works against National Socialist use of the *Nibelungenlied* in the final years of the Second World War to promote the ideal of a nation-state founded on absolute individual obedience to the supreme authority figures under even the most hopeless of circumstances (*SfeS*, p. 153). Fühmann's characterisation of this misinterpretation as the 'Nach-Stalingrad-Phase' in National Socialist reception of the epic refers to Hermann Göring's January 1943 speech in which he likened the hopelessly outnumbered German troops in Stalingrad to the Nibelungs' 'Kampf ohnegleichen' to the last man in the burning banqueting hall.[13] In the screenplay, Fühmann comprehensively distances this episode from Göring's infamous misappropriation of it by declining to depict the events in the burning banqueting hall at all. Instead, the viewer only sees their aftermath before the final battle: 'der Innenhof vor dem ausgebrannten, noch qualmenden Festsaal. Der Hof liegt voller Leichname, umgekommen durchs Schwert wie durchs Feuer. Die ausgebrannte Halle scheint leer' (*DNN*, p. 135). It is also striking that Fühmann uses animated rather than live-action footage in his depiction of this battle, which clearly distances this episode from the live-action scenes surrounding it and presents it in an ironic light by subtly suggesting that it may be a fictional invention. Additionally, Fühmann's stage direction 'Wie klein diese Menschlein doch erscheinen!', and the emphasis that he places on the Burgundians' 'Marionettenhaftigkeit' (both *DNN*, p. 135), ironically distances this episode from Göring's perverse parallel between the Wehrmacht and the Nibelungs by deflating the heroic status that Göring ascribed to the combatants. Furthermore, Fühmann's description of the final battle as a 'kurzes Getümmel' (*DNN*, p. 135) during which Volker and Gernot are slain before Hagen and Gunther are overpowered mocks Göring's presentation of this episode as an unparalleled heroic fight to the last man. This is underlined by the term *Getümmel*'s status

---

[13] Hermann Goering's speech of 18 January 1943, in Dietrich Möller, 'Geschichte aktuell' (18 November 2002), (accessed 11/05/2024).

as 'auszerordentlich beliebt [...] für kampf- und schlachtszenen', reflected by the long list of examples of its usage in this sense from Luther to Hebbel.[14] Fühmann's concerted efforts outlined above to shift the battle into a lower register make it appear much less uniquely elevated than National Socialist interpretations of it suggest and thus distance this episode from National Socialist misuse of it to promote ideologies which idealised war and violence.

Furthermore, Fühmann assumes a clear distance from earlier, underlying National Socialist misappropriations of the *Nibelungenlied* as a 'national epic' promoting the ideal of an ethnically and linguistically homogeneous Germanic nation-state and lamenting the 'betrayal' of idealised 'Nordic' characters such as Siegfried by 'ethnically inferior' 'Dinaric' characters such as Hagen by explicitly confronting National Socialist use of these terms in relation to the epic (*SfeS*, p. 153). In the screenplay, Fühmann confounds this National Socialist racial binary with an ethnically and linguistically diverse cast of characters, which, he states in his film proposal, will need to be reflected by an equally diverse casting of actors, stressing that the Huns and Icelanders – especially Brunhild – should be played by non-German actors (*SfeS*, p. 161). Incidentally, throughout the film, Fühmann spells Brünhild's name as 'Brynhild', drawing her closer to her incarnation as 'Brynhildr' in the Icelandic Edda cycle and working against National Socialist attempts to easily familiarise and appropriate her as a 'German' character.

Fühmann's insistence that the Huns should be played by non-Germans also distances them from National Socialist portrayals of them as sub-human by typecasting them for a sense of foreignness which embodied 'the very prototype of the barbarian'.[15] Fühmann achieves this by no longer presenting them as jabbering away in 'incomprehensible language' as they do in Fritz Lang's 1924 film adaptation,

---

[14] DWB 6 (1898) s.v. www.woerterbuchnetz.de/DWB/getümmel.

[15] Brüggen, Elke and Holznagel, Franz-Josef, '*Des künic Etzelen man*: The Huns and their King in Fritz Lang's Classic Silent Film Die Nibelungen and in the Nibelungenlied', *Thamyris/Intersecting*, Nr. 29 (2015), p. 223.

instead providing them with distinctive voices which create linguistic diversity in the script and force the viewer to assume a critical distance to their preconceptions of the epic. For example, the stage directions in I,2 state that 'Einer der Hunnen wendet sich *in hunnischer Sprache* an Rüdiger und fragt, ob das vor ihnen Worms sei, ein ungewohntes Wort, das ihm schwer über die Zunge geht.' (*DNN*, p. 12; my emphasis). The unusual sound of the German place name 'Worms' when the Hunnish rider attempts to pronounce it creates defamiliarisation through placing aural distance between the German-speaking viewer and an otherwise familiar place name. This defamiliarisation is further reinforced by the stage direction, 'Wir blicken mit den hunnischen Edlen auf die Stadt' (*DNN*, p. 12), which forces the viewer to view the film's familiar German setting from a non-German perspective. Furthermore, Rüdiger's reply to the Hun in Hunnish is particularly striking because it reveals him to be a much less unequivocally 'German' character than previous nationalist representations of him seemed to suggest. According to Grosse and Rautenberg, the character of Rüdiger had inspired eight spin-off tragedies between 1849 and 1939, including Felix Dahn's *Markgraf Rüdeger von Bechelaren* (1875) and the 1939 drama *Rüdiger von Bechelaren* by Hans Baumann, a National Socialist now best known for composing the German Labour Front anthem. Although it is unclear whether Fühmann was aware of these specific dramas, both authors' ideologically problematic historical novels had previously enjoyed huge popularity. Fühmann's conscious presentation of Rüdiger as transcending the divide between 'German' and 'Hun' thus most likely works against broader nationalist appropriation of the epic by such well-known earlier authors. Moreover, it is significant that the first words spoken in the film are not in German; instead, they form the end of the Latin *Gloria in excelsis deo* (*SfeS*, p. 11) – the international *lingua franca* of what Ernst Robert Curtius termed the 'Latin Middle Ages'. This has the effect of lifting the screenplay's plot out of the exclusively German context in which previous nationalist versions had presented it and recontextualising it within the broader framework of thirteenth-century Central European society.

Fühmann's consistent emphasis on the internationality and diversity of the *Nibelungenlied* thus underlines the 'räumliche Weite' of the epic, countering aggressively nationalist Third Reich versions with a version which reflects the 'international character of socialist ideology'[16] and justifies its reintegration into GDR cultural heritage. This superseding of the inward-looking nationalisms previously associated with the *Nibelungenlied* is most clearly exemplified by Fühmann's presentation of Etzel's kingdom, a multi-ethnic state which brings together 'Herren und Damen aller Hautfarben und Rassenphysiognomien; es kann auf der Welt keine Gala und keine – weltlichen wie geistlichen – Würdenzeichen geben, die hier nicht vertreten wären' (*DNN*, p. 105). In the *Szenarium für einen Spielfilm*, Fühmann describes his presentation of Etzel's kingdom as an ideal higher order bringing together many different peoples in a spirit of tolerance and peace 'in der sich eine Einheit von ritterlicher Ethik und Staatsmacht verkörpert' (SfeS, p. 159). The 'unity' that Fühmann evokes as the lasting impression of Etzel's kingdom at the end of this section of his film proposal reveals that such a structure of society would enable a synthesis of the dialectic between the 'ethical imperatives' governing individuals' personal conduct and the 'power of the state' governing public and political conduct (*SfeS*, p. 159). He suggests that this would enable its citizens to become successful classconscious citizens (*SfeS*, p. 159) – provided that its leaders were experienced in resisting intrigues and its army were strong enough to defend it from warlike enemies (*SfeS*, p. 159) – clearly establishing this apparently utopian situation as something to be worked towards which can be realised under the right social and political conditions.

Der Nibelunge Not thus represents a radical rejection of existing concepts of the *Nibelungenlied* as a foundational epic on the level of the *Iliad* for the German nation. In the screenplay, Fühmann pursues an innovative approach to recovering the *Nibelungenlied* from its comparative obscurity in the GDR against the backdrop of contemporary debates surrounding what constituted the foundation of cultural heritage for the East German state and the role that this heritage should

---

[16] Spiewok, 'Zur Erbediskussion', p. 91.

play in the everyday life of the nation. He parses apart the pre-feudal / heroic and feudal / courtly layers of the epic, revealing just how anachronistic he perceives the individualistic behaviour of Siegfried to be within a structure of society that increasingly favours the collective over the individual. He also works against National Socialist appropriation of the epic which promoted a form of nationalism based on militaristic violence, racist notions of ethnic homogeneity, and blind, suicidal loyalty to supreme leaders governing the state. Instead, he suggests how this epic could be rehabilitated and reintegrated into the cultural heritage of the GDR to promote peace, human dignity, and co-operation between social groups to establish a collective founded on these values. In this way, as Peter Göhler suggests, Fühmann's adaptation of *Der Nibelunge Not* makes the epic 'untauglich […] für seine Einvernahme für Gewalt und schauerliche Verherrlichung von Totschlag, Mord und Krieg'[17] for which it had been misused as a foundational text by nationalists and National Socialists alike.

---

[17] Göhler, Peter, 'Fühmanns Filmentwurf Der Nibelunge Not', Paul Alfred Kleinert (ed.), *Franz Fühmanns Filmwelten* (Leipzig: Engelsdorfer Verlag, 2022), p. 87.

Appendix: Epic Beginnings

The quotations are sorted in chronological order, based mainly on books chosen for the exhibition; in brackets the catalogue sections.

Iliad

μῆνιν ἄειδε θεὰ Πηληϊάδεω Ἀχιλῆος
οὐλομένην, ἣ μυρί᾽ Ἀχαιοῖς ἄλγε᾽ ἔθηκε,
πολλὰς δ᾽ ἰφθίμους ψυχὰς Ἄϊδι προΐαψεν
ἡρώων, αὐτοὺς δὲ ἑλώρια τεῦχε κύνεσσιν
οἰωνοῖσί τε πᾶσι, Διὸς δ᾽ ἐτελείετο βουλή,
ἐξ οὗ δὴ τὰ πρῶτα διαστήτην ἐρίσαντε
Ἀτρεΐδης τε ἄναξ ἀνδρῶν καὶ δῖος Ἀχιλλεύς.

Homeri Opera in five vols, OUP 1920
online as part of the Perseus Project.

Sing, o göttliche singe den zorn des Peliden, der unheil
Ueber die Griechen gehäuft, die helden zum Orcus gesendet,
Und die körper zum aas den hunden und vögeln gegeben;
Dadnrch [!] wurde der willen des obersten Gottes erfüllet,
Als Achilles und Agamemnon, der könig der schaaren,
Streit gewannen und zwietracht der beiden herzen zertrennte.

Bodmer 1767 (section 1), p. 159.

Singe den Zorn, o Göttin, des Peleiaden Achilleus,
Ihn, der entbrannt den Achaiern unnennbaren Jammer erregte,
Und viel tapfere Seelen der Heldensöhne zum Ais
Sendete, aber sie selber zum Raub' ausstreckte den Hunden,
Und dem Gevögel umher: so ward Zeus Wille vollendet:
Seit dem Tag', als einst durch bitteren Zank sich entzweiten
Atreus Sohn, der Herrscher des Volks, und der edle Achilleus.

Voß 1844 (section 3), vol. 1, p. 3.

Of Peleus' son, Achilles, sing, O Muse,
The vengeance, deep and deadly; whence to Greece
Unnumber'd ills arose; which many a soul
Of mighty warriors to the viewless shades

Untimely sent; they on the battle plain
Unburied lay, a prey to rav'ning dogs,
And carrion birds; but so Heav'n decreed,
From that sad day when first in wordy war,
The mighty Agamemnon, king of men,
Confronted stood by Peleus' godlike son.
> Lord Stanley 1862 (section 2), p. 1.

In uralten Zeiten wohnten auf der Insel Samothrace, im ägäischen Meere, zwei Brüder, Jasion und Dardanus, Söhne des Jupiter und einer Nymphe, Fürsten des Landes.
> Schwab 1882 (section 3), beginning of 'Die Sagen Troja's'.

Sing, o Göttin, von Zorn, von des Peleussohnes Achilleus
Heillosem Zorn, der unsägliches Leid den Achäern gestiftet,
Der viel tapfere Seelen zu Hades niedergesendet,
Seelen der Helden, indes er sie selber den Hunden zum Raube
Schuf und den Vögeln zum Frass, – so gieng Zeus Rat in Erfüllung,
Seit dem Tag, da zuerst sich die Beiden in Hader entzweiten
Atreus Sohn, der Gebieter des Heers und der hehre Achilleus.
> Fick 1902 (section 2), p. 1.

In der Odyssee habe ich euch erzählt, daß die Griechen in den Krieg nach Troja mußten, weil Paris dem König Menelaos die Frau geraubt hatte. Ein Stück von dem Kriege will ich euch nun erzählen. Die Griechen hatten schon lange um Troja gekämpft. Mal hatten die Griechen gesiegt und mal die Troer. Aber die Griechen hatten Troja nicht zerstören können, denn soweit waren sie nie gekommen. Deswegen war der Krieg noch immer nicht zu Ende.
> Otto 1904 (section 5), p. 1.

In the deep forest that clothes Mound Ida, not far from the strong city of Troy, Paris, son of King Priam, watched his father's flocks by night.
> Lang n.d. (section 5), p. 1.

Once upon a time there was a certain King of Sparta who had a most beautiful daughter, Helen by name. There was not a prince in Greece but wished to marry her.
> Church 1908 (section 6), p. 15.

Singe, Göttin, den Zorn des Peleiaden Achilleus,
Der zum Verhängnis unendliche Leiden schuf den Achaiern
Und die Seelen so vieler gewaltiger Helden zum Hades
Sandte, aber sie selbst zum Raub den Hunden gewährte
Und den Vögeln zum Fraß – so wurde der Wille Kronions
Endlich erfüllt –, nachdem sich einmal im Zwiste geschieden
Atreus' Sohn, der Herrscher des Volks, und der edle Achilleus.

> Voß/Rupé 1922 (section 2), p. 1.

To the ancient Greeks the Siege of Troy was the greatest and most important event in the Age of Heroes – that age of wonder when the Immortals who dwelt on Olympus and whom they worshipped as gods, mingled with mankind and took a visible part in their affairs.

> Green 1965 (section 5), p. 10.

Singe uns, Göttin, vom Zorn des Peleus-Sohnes Achilleus,
Der unendliches Leid hat den Achaiern gebracht.
Vieler Helden Seelen hat er zum Hades gesendet,
Während er ihren Leib Hunden und Vögeln zum Fraß
Liegen ließ, daß sich erfüllte der Wille des Vaters der Götter.
Denn in schrecklichem Zwist hatten sich bitter entzweit
Atreus' Sohn, der Beherrscher des Volks, und der edle Achilleus.

> Hoepke 1977 (section 5), p. 9.

In a small kingdom in the north of Greece ruled Peleus, king of Phthia, who was much favoured by the gods. When he was no longer young, he fell in love with the sea-goddess Thetis, daughter of blue-haired and blue-bearded Nereus, who dwelt in the depths of the Aegean Sea, together with his consort, Doris, and their fifty daughters.

> Picard 1986 (section 5), p. 1.

This is the story of a bitter quarrel between two proud and powerful men. It brought death to hundreds of brave heroes and destroyed one of the great cities of the world. And yet it started with something very small … It all began with an apple.

> Cross 2012 (section 4), p. 11.

Now that I'm dead I know everything. This is what I wished would happen, but like so many of my wishes it failed to come true. I know only a few factoids that I didn't know before. Death is much too high a price to pay for the satisfaction of curiosity, needless to say.

>   Atwood 2018 (section 6), p. 1.

Troy. The most marvellous kingdom in all the world. The Jewel of the Aegean. Glittering Ilium, the city that rose and fell not once but twice. Gatekeeper of traffic in and out of the barbarous east. Kingdom of gold and horses. Fierce nurse of prophets, princes, heroes, warriors and poets. Under the protection of ARES, ARTEMIS, APOLLO and APHRODITE she stood for years as the paragon of all that can be achieved in the arts of war and peace, trade and treaty, love and art, statecraft, piety and civil harmony. When she fell, a hole opened in the human world that may never be filled, save in memory. Poets must sing the story over and over again, passing it from generation to generation, lest in losing Troy we lose a part of ourselves.

>   Fry 2020 (section 3), p. 1.

44 Appendix

Odyssey

ἄνδρα μοι ἔννεπε, μοῦσα, πολύτροπον, ὃς μάλα πολλὰ
πλάγχθη, ἐπεὶ Τροίης ἱερὸν πτολίεθρον ἔπερσεν·
πολλῶν δ' ἀνθρώπων ἴδεν ἄστεα καὶ νόον ἔγνω,
πολλὰ δ' ὅ γ' ἐν πόντῳ πάθεν ἄλγεα ὃν κατὰ θυμόν,
ἀρνύμενος ἥν τε ψυχὴν καὶ νόστον ἑταίρων.

Homer, *Odyssey*, ed. by William Heinemann 1919
online as part of the Perseus Project.

Sage mir, Muse, die Thaten des vielgewanderten Mannes,
Welcher so weit geirrt, nach der heiligen Troja Zerstörung,
Vieler Menschen Städte gesehn, und Sitte gelernt hat,
Und auf dem Meere so viel' unnennbare Leiden erduldet,
Seine Seele zu retten, und seiner Freunde Zurückkunft.
Aber die Freunde rettet' er nicht, wie eifrig er strebte;
Denn sie bereiteten selbst durch Missethat ihr Verderben:
Thoren! welche die Rinder des hohen Sonnenbeherschers
Schlachteten; siehe, der Gott nahm ihnen den Tag der Zurückkunft.
Sage hievon auch uns ein weniges, Tochter Kronions.

Voß 1781 (section 2), p. 9.

Melde den Mann mir, Muse, den Vielgewandten, der vielfach
Umgeirrt, als Troja, die heilige Stadt, er zerstöret;
Vieler Menschen Städte geseh'n, und Sitte gelernt hat,
Auch im Meere so viel herzkrankende Leiden erduldet,
Strebend für seine Seele zugleich und der Freunde Zurückkunft.
Nicht die Freunde jedoch errettet' er, eifrig bemüht zwar;
Denn sie bereiteten selbst durch Missethat ihr Verderben:
Thörichte, welche die Rinder dem leuchtenden Sohn Hyperions
Schlachteten; jener darauf nahm ihnen den Tag der Zurückkunft.
Hievon sag' auch uns ein Weniges, Tochter Kronions.

Voß 1844 (section 3), vol. 2, p. 1.

Odysseus war der Sohn des Laertes und König von Ithaka. Er war weit berühmt wegen seiner Klugheit und Tapferkeit. Er war auch schon verheiratet und hatte einen kleinen Sohn, den Telemach. Da mußten plötzlich alle Griechen in den Krieg. Paris, der Sohn des Königs Priamos, hatte die Frau des Königs Menelaos geraubt. Die war das schönste Weib bei den Menschen. Sie hieß Helena. Menelaos wollte seine Frau natürlich wieder haben und bat nun die anderen Griechen, ihm zu helfen. Sie wollten das gern, denn wer hilft wohl nicht gern seinen Nachbarn?

Otto 1903 (section 4), p. 1.

In the days of long ago there reigned over Ithaca, a rugged little island in the sea to the west of Greece, a king whose name was Odysseus. Odysseus feared no man. Stronger and braver than other men was he, wiser, and more full of clever devices. Far and wide he was known as Odysseus of the many counsels. Wise, also, was his queen, Penelope, and she was as fair as she was wise; and as good as she was fair.

Lang n.d. (section 4), p. 1.

A great many years ago there was a very famous siege of a city called Troy.

Church 1907 (section 6), p. 15.

This is the story of Odysseus, the most renowned of all the heroes the Greek poets have told us of – of Odysseus, his wars and wanderings. And this story of Odysseus begins with his son, the youth who was called Telemachus.

Colum 1920 (section 6), p. 3.

This history tells of the wanderings of Ulysses and his followers in their return from Troy, after the destruction of that famous city of Asia by the Grecians. He was inflamed with desire of seeing again, after ten years' absence, his wife and native country Ithaca.

Lamb 1926 (section 4), p. 7.

Muse, erzähle uns von jenem gewaltigen Helden,
Der die Stadt Troja zerstört, der dann irrte umher,
Viele Menschen und Städte sah, auf Wogen des Meeres
Schmerzen und Leiden ertrug! Immer war er besorgt
Um das eigene Leben und um die Heimkehr der Freunde.
War er auch noch so bemüht – dennoch gelang's ihm nicht.
Denn sie gingen zugrunde durch ihren eigenen Frevel.
Rinder des Helios hatten sie umgebracht.
Deshalb versagte der zornige Gott die Stunde der Heimkehr.
Davon erzähle uns, Muse, soviel Du weißt!

Hoepke 1975 (section 4), p. 11.

After their ten-year-long war with the men of Troy was ended and the Trojan city had fallen in flames and smoke, the victorious Greeks gathered together their booty and their prisoners; and when the great King Agamemnon, who was in charge of all the Grecian host, had given the word, one by one all those leaders of the Greeks who had survived the fighting boarded their ships and set sail for home.

Picard 1986 (section 5), p. 215.

Nibelungenlied

Uns ist in alten mæren wunders vil geseit
von helden lobebæren, von grôzer arebeit,
von freuden hôchgezîten, von weinen und von klagen,
von küener recken strîten muget ir nû wunder hœren sagen.
> Das Nibelungenlied, ed. Karl Bartsch 1866
> on google books from Taylorian Vet.Ger.III.B.552.
> On display: Ed. Bartsch/de Boor 1988 (section 3), p. 3.

Eh die aonischen Musen in Deutschlands hainen gewandelt,
Als Achilles noch nicht in deutschen gesängen gefochten,
Und Ulysses die freyer noch nicht im bettler betrogen,
Sangen die Eschilbache, von deutschen Musen begeistert,
Eigne gesänge, die frucht des selbst erfindenden geistes.
Einer von ihnen sang mit Mäonides tone die schwester,
Welcher die brüder den theueen [sic] gemahl erschlugen, die schwester
Wieder die brüder erschlug. Die zeit hat den nahmen getilget,
Aber sein lied gerettet, ich hab' es gehört, und ich will es
Lauter singen, es soll vom Rhein zur Ostsee ertönen.
> Bodmer 1767 (section 1), p. 309.

In ancient song and story marvels high are told,
Of knights of high emprize, and adventures manifold;
Of joy and merry feasting; of lamenting, woe, and fear;
Of champions' bloody battles many marvels shall ye hear.
> *Illustrations of Northern Antiquities, From the Earlier Teuronic and Scandinavian Romances; Being an Abstract of the Book of Heroes and Nibelungen Lay* […], [ed. by H. W. Weber, R. Jamieson, and Sir W. Scott.] Edinburgh 1814, p. 167.

Uns ist in alten Mären des Wunders viel gesagt
Von Helden, reich an Ehren, in Mühsal unverzagt.
Von Freude und Festzeiten, von Weinen und von Klagen,
Von kühner Recken Streiten mögt ihr nun Wunder hören sagen.
> Marbach 1840 (section 5), n. pag.

Uns ist in alten Mären Wunders viel gesait
Von Helden, werth der Ehren, von großer Kühnheit;

48   Appendix

Von Freuden und Hochgezeiten, von Weinen und von Klagen,
Von kühner Recken Streiten mögt Ihr nun Wunder hören sagen.
> Pfizer 1843 (section 4), p. 1.

Legends of bygone times reveal wonders and prodigies,
Of heroes worthy endless fame, – of matchless braveries, –
Of jubilees and festal sports, – of tears and sorrows great, –
And knights who daring combats fought: the like I now relate.
> *Das Nibelungen Lied; or, Lay of the Last Nibelungers*, translated into English verse after Carl Lachmann's collated and corrected text by Jonathan Birch, Berlin 1848, p. 1

The Lay of the Nibelungen princes! What is it? A strange, wild story, full of weird beauty and god-like heroism, like the gleams of light in a Salvator landscape, with a background of storm and darkness. The old, old story of woman's passionate love, and impulsive forgetfulness of consequences; of man's protecting tenderness and chivalrous daring; but true knight and queenly woman alike falling victims to the bad man, with the indomitable will, who comes before us as a grotesque mockery of humanity, endowed with all subtlety of intellect, but having a fossilized heart.
> Hands 1880 (section 6), p. 1.

In old tales they tell us many wonders of heroes and of high courage, of glad feasting, of wine and of mourning; and herein ye shall read of the marvellous deeds and of the strife of brave men.
> Armour 1897 (section 6), p. 1.

Long, long ago, in the kingdom of Burgundy, there lived a princess named Kriemhilda, whose beauty, gentleness, and virtue were famed throughout the land. Her father had died during her early maidenhood, and since that unhappy day she had resided with her mother under the safe protection of her three brothers – Gunther, Gernot, and Giselher.
> Anon. 1907 (section 4), p. 9.

Siegfried was born a Prince and grew to be a hero, a hero with a heart of gold. Though he could fight, and was as strong as any lion, yet he could love too and be as gentle as a child.
> MacGregor 1908 (section 4), p. 1.

Epic Beginnings 49

Long ago, comrades, brave things were seen in this city. For the old king, whom men called Dankrat, had driven back his enemies, as the wind scatters the thunder-clouds; and now in his old age he lived rich and in peace wirh his noble wife Uté, his little daughter Kriemhild, and his three sons.

    Anon. 1911 (section 6), p. 7.

Siegfried was a great and noble prince whose fame, by reason of his mighty deeds, hath endurance through the Ages. His sire was King Siegmund of the Netherlands and his mother was named Sigelinde. Ere yet he had reached the years that are mellowed by wisdom, Siegfried was of proud and haughty spirit and brooked not restraint. Great was his strength, and if his playfellows obeyed not his will in all things, he smote them harshly, so that the hated as much as they feared him. Wild and wilful was the prince as a lad may be.

    Mackenzie 1912 (section 6), p. 354.

Im Burgunderlande wuchs ein edles Mädchen auf, es mochte wohl im ganzen Lande kein schöneres geben. Kriemhild hieß sie und gedieh zu einem herrlichen Weibe, um das dereinst viele edle Helden ihr Leben verlieren sollten. Sie war im ganzen Lande beliebt, und ihre keusche Sitte galt allen Frauen zum Vorbilde. Drei reiche, mächtige Fürsten, Gunther, Gernot und Giselher, welches ihre Brüder waren, betreuten sie.

    Wägner/Heichen 1943 (section 5), p. 83.

Viel Staunenswertes ist in den alten Geschichten auf uns gekommen: Kunde von hochberühmten Helden und ihren Taten und ihrer Not, von Festesfreuden und Jammergeschrei und den Kämpfen der Kühnen, und wer mag, kann nun von all dem hören, es werden aber wundersame Dinge darunter sein.

    Fühmann 2005 (section 3), p. 6.

fliederung dunkler fluff – tüpfel
sehe schuss siena gebrannt um flügel
karmin karneol spüre herzschlag siena
flirres gespan klöppel der schwinge
luftwärts gebannt unter eines körpers
flitsch
  – fahre auf

    Draesner 2016 (section 4), p. 5.

Exhibition Catalogues

Taylorian: Epic! Homer and the *Nibelungenlied* in Translation curated by MARY BOYLE and PHILIP FLACKE

1. Epic?

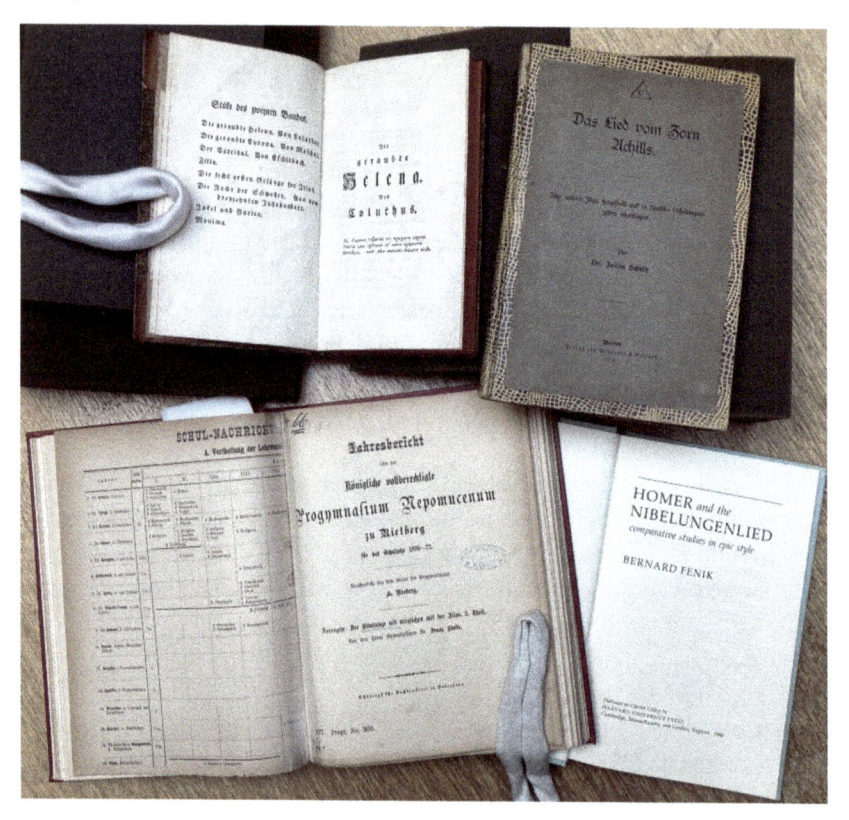

Illustration 11: Section 1. From top to bottom, left to right: Bodmer 1767, Schultz 1901, Stolte 1877, Fenik 1986. Photograph: Philip Flacke

'Dieses Gedicht hat etwas iliadisches' – 'There is something *Iliad*-like about this poem'. With these words, in 1757, the Swiss critic Johann Jakob Bodmer set the tone for public perceptions of the *Nibelungenlied* for years to come. The thirteenth-century German epic had been rediscovered just two years earlier, and Bodmer was its first editor, though he only printed a section of the text. In the course of his work, he thoroughly reshaped the material according to his own theories on epic. This was informed by his collaboration with Johann Jakob Breitinger, in which the two men had already laid the groundwork for a new understanding of Homer, focusing less on authoritative rules than on supposed original 'genius'. The mid-eighteenth century thus marks the starting point for a shared reception of both Homer and the *Nibelungenlied*.

Reading, translating, and adapting either text has often meant invoking the other. Not only has the *Nibelungenlied* been adapted in the metre of Homer, the hexameter, but Homer, too, has been translated in ways that imitate the form of the *Nibelungenlied*. Labelling the story of Siegfried and Kriemhild a 'German *Iliad*' became a trope, and not just in the German-speaking world, but in the anglophone world as well. When William Morris wrote of 'the Great Story of the North, which should be to all our race what the Tale of Troy was to the Greeks', he was referring primarily to the Old Norse *Völsunga Saga*, but this was often incorporated into English-language retellings of the *Nibelungenlied*, particularly where it was felt that there were gaps in the narrative. The supposed connection between the Nibelungen material and Homer also reached the United States where, in 1892, a school reader entitled *The Story of the German Iliad*, taught sixth- and seventh-grade students about the 'Rhine-gold', Siegfried's death and Kriemhilda's revenge.

In the academic world, Homer and the *Nibelungenlied* have sometimes been the subject of comparative study to this day. This got its second wind, when in the 1930s, the American Classicist Milman Parry and his pupil Albert B. Lord developed their theories on the specifics of so-called 'oral poetry'. They had studied the living tradition of Serbo-Croatian *guslars* in order to better understand the development and transmission of the Homeric epics. But their findings have since also been linked to the *Nibelungenlied*.

1757 *Chriemhilden Rache, und Die Klage; Zwey Heldengedichte. Aus dem schvväbischen Zeitpuncte samt Fragmenten aus dem Gedichte von den Nibelungen und aus dem Josaphat*, [ed. by Johann Jacob Bodmer], Zürich.
Taylor Institution Library: ARCH.8o.G.1757

In the first modern edition of the *Nibelungenlied*, the text has undergone major changes. Bodmer cut about two thirds, presenting only the last part with the Burgundians at the court of Kriemhild's second husband Etzel and Kriemhild's revenge for the death of Siegfried together with 'fragments' from the first two thirds. This drastic interference with the text is part of an attempt to make it more like the *Iliad*.

> All these passages I have cut out and, I believe, with the same legitimacy as Homer when he left out Helen's abduction, Iphigenia's sacrifice, and all the events of the ten years preceding the dispute between Achilles and Agamemnon, to which he only refers on occasion as to something generally known.
>
> (Alle diese Stücke habe ich abgeschnitten, und ich glaube mit demselben Rechte, mit welchem Homer die Entführung der Helena, die Aufopferung der Iphigenia, und alle Begegnisse der zehn Jahre, die vor dem Zwiste zwischen Achilles und Agamemnon vorhergegangen sind, weggelassen hat, auf die er nur bey Gelegenheiten sich als auf bekannte Sachen beziehet.)

Other aspects in which the *Nibelungenlied* resembles Homer according to Bodmer include the different facets of bravery in various heroes, the variety of battle scenes, and the immediacy with which the poet immerses his audience in the action. As to the first two thirds of the *Nibelungenlied*, Bodmer sees 'no indication that it will ever be printed in its entirety.' ('Man siehet keinen Anschein, daß er jemals werde ganz gedrukt werden.').

Directly following his translation of the first six books of the *Iliad* – an early attempt of adapting the original metric form of Homer's metre, the hexameter – Bodmer printed a text he called '*The Sister's Revenge.*' It is his loose hexametric translation of the last third of the *Nibelungenlied*, the same passage he had singled out for his edition of the Middle High German text a decade earlier.

1767 'Die Ersten Gesänge der Ilias', in [Johann Jakob] Bodmer: *Calliope*, vol. 2. (Zürich), pp. 157–306; *and* 'Die Rache der Schwester', in [Johann Jakob] Bodmer: *Calliope*, vol. 2. (Zürich), pp. 307–72.
Taylor Institution Library: FINCH.U.271

Bodmer continues his ongoing mission of altering the *Nibelungenlied* in order to harmonise it with his ideas about Homer. This involves adding a proem, a form of verse prologue. Styling himself as the singer of another writer's song, Bodmer does not invoke the Muses, goddesses of inspiration. But he alludes to them – to the Greek Muses of Mount Helicon ('Aonien' being a mythical name for Boeotia) as well as to 'German Muses', who used to inspire the poets of the Middle Ages like Wolfram von Eschenbach ('die Eschilbache'). What is more, according to Bodmer's proem, the nameless poet of the *Nibelungenlied* sang 'in the tune' of Homer himself (called 'Mäonides' after his supposed homeland Maeonia or ancestor Maeon).

> Before the Aonian Muses walked in the groves of Germany, when Achilles had not yet fought in German songs and Ulysses not yet deceived the suitors in the guise of a beggar, the Eschilbachs, inspired by German Muses, sang their own songs, the fruit of the spirit that invents on its own. One of them sang, in the tune of Maeonides, about the sister whose dear husband was killed by her brothers; the sister in turn killed the brothers. Time has extinguished his name but preserved his song. I have heard it and intend to sing it louder. It shall resound from the Rhine to the Baltic Sea.

> (Eh die aonischen Musen in Deutschlands hainen gewandelt,
> Als Achilles noch nicht in deutschen gesängen gefochten,
> Und Ulysses die freyer noch nicht im bettler betrogen,
> Sangen die Eschilbache, von deutschen Musen begeistert,
> Eigne gesänge, die frucht des selbst erfindenden geistes.
> Einer von ihnen sang mit Mäonides tone die schwester,
> Welcher die brüder den theuen [!] gemahl erschlugen, die schwester
> Wieder die brüder erschlug. Die zeit hat den nahmen getilget,
> Aber sein lied gerettet, ich hab' es gehört, und ich will es
> Lauter singen, es soll vom Rhein zur Ostsee ertönen.)

54 Catalogue

1877 Franz Stolte, 'Der Nibelunge nôt verglichen mit der Ilias. 2. Theil', in *Jahresbericht über das Königliche vollberechtigte Progymnasium Nepomucenum zu Rietberg* (Schuljahr 1876–77), pp. 3–27.
Taylor Institution Library: REP.G.3483 (1–20)

1901 *Das Lied vom Zorn Achills,* aus unserer Ilias hergestellt und in deutsche Nibelungenzeilen übertragen von Julius Schultz, Berlin.
Private loan

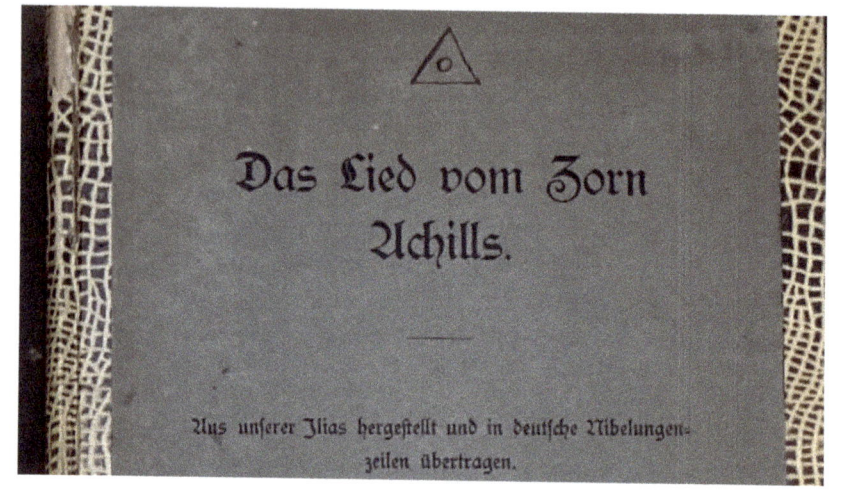

Illustration 12: Censorship mark on Schultz (1901)

The symbol on the cover of a circle or zero inside a triangle was used by the *Oberkommando in den Marken*, a Berlin military authority, to mark books and documents that had passed censorship in World War I. Thanks go to the art historian Holger Birkholz in Dresden, for providing this information.

1986 Bernard Fenik, *Homer and the Nibelungenlied: comparative studies in epic style*, Cambridge, MA.
Taylor Institution Library: EB.610.A.12

2. Translating Verse

Illustration 13: Section 2. From top to bottom: Lord Stanley 1862, Bürger 1776, Voß 1777, Voß 1781, Voß 1780, Voß 1790, Voß/Rupé 1922. Photograph: Philip Flacke

Enthusiasm for the Homeric epics reached new heights in the second half of the eighteenth century, when we come to a new chapter in their German translation. Various young poets, taking their cue from Bodmer and Herder, began work on a German text that was supposed to move its audience in the same way that the original Greek did. To these poets, translation was to a considerable extent a question of metrics. Numerous renderings of extracts of both the *Iliad* and the *Odyssey* were published alongside discussions on prosody and versification, documenting the search for a German Homer.

Earlier critics like Johann Christoph Gottsched had favoured the iambic alexandrine, which followed the literary model of France and had long been supposed to suit the German speech rhythm better than dactyls and spondees. Rejecting the alexandrine in many cases now meant rejecting the exemplary role of French. Gottfried August Bürger explicitly aimed to make Homer 'an old German' ('da ich den Homer in der Übersetzung gleichsam zum alten Deutschen gemacht wissen möchte') and chose iambic pentameter. Friedrich Leopold Stolberg and Johann Heinrich Voss on the other hand, who knew both Bürger and one another from their time at university in Göttingen, aimed to imitate Homer's own metre in German: the hexameter.

Voss went on to publish full translations of the *Odyssey* in 1781 and of the *Iliad* in 1793. His text set a new standard for German writers of hexametric verse in years to come and remains the most influential German translation of Homer to this day. Even a twentieth-century bilingual edition for educated readers like the one in the *Tempel-Klassiker* series presents the German text in a revised version of Voss.

1776 'Homers Iliade. Fünfte Rhapsodie', verdeutscht von Gottfried August Bürger, in *Deutsches Museum* 1776, 1. Stück, pp. 4–14; *and* 'Der Iliade Homers zwanzigster Gesang', verdeutscht durch Friedrich Leopold Graf zu Stolberg, in *Deutsches Museum* 1776, 11. Stück, pp. 957–82. Taylor Institution Library: VET.PER. 1777

1777 'Odüsseus Erzählung von den Küklopen. Aus dem neunten Gesange der Odüssee Homers', übersetzt von Johann Heinrich Voß, in *Deutsches Museum* 1777, 5. Stück, pp. 462–78.
Taylor Institution Library: VET.PER. 1777

1780 'Ueber Ortügia. Aus dem 15 Ges. der Odüssee' von Johann Heinrich Voß, in *Deutsches Museum* 1780, 4. Stück, pp. 302–12.
Taylor Institution Library: VET.PER. 1780

1781 *Homers Odüßee*, übersetzt von Johann Heinrich Voß, Hamburg.
Private loan

1790 'Probe der Vossischen Ilias', [translated by Johann Heinrich Voß], in *Neues Deutsches Museum* 2, 1. Stück, pp. 1–43.
Taylor Institution Library: VET.PER. Bd.2 (1790: Jan./Jun.)

1862 [Edward Smith-Stanley, 14th Earl of Derby], *Translations of Poems, Ancient and Modern Not Published*, London.
Taylor Institution Library: FIEDLER.A.150

Lord Stanley is the only British Prime Minister so far to have translated Homer's *Iliad*. His take on its first book is included in this volume, of which, according to the dedication, only a few copies were printed for friends. On his choice of metre he writes 'that, if justice is ever to be done to the easy flow and majestic simplicity of the grand old Poet, it can only be in the heroic blank verse'. He writes more extensively on the matter in the preface to his full translation of the *Iliad* that was to follow two years later and appeared in several editions:

> Numerous as have been the translators of the Iliad, or of parts of it, the metres which have been selected have been almost as various: the ordinary couplet in rhyme, the Spenserian stanza, the Trochaic or Ballad metre, all have had their partisans, even to that 'pestilent heresy' of the so-called English Hexameter; a metre wholly repugnant to the genius of our language; which can only be pressed into the service by a violation of every rule of prosody; and of which, notwithstanding my respect for the eminent men who have attempted to naturalize it, I could never read ten lines without being

irresistibly reminded of Canning's 'Dactylics call'st thou them? God help thee, silly one!'

1861 *Homer's Gedichte*, im Versmaße der Urschrift übersetzt von Karl Uschner, in zwei Theilen, erster Theil: Ilias, zweiter Theil: Odyssee, Berlin.
Taylor Institution Library: 1.B.21 (two volumes in one)

While Lord Stanley might have deemed the 'English hexameter' a 'pestilent heresy', the German Karl Uschner undertook a new translation of Homer 'in the original metre' – which is to say, in hexameter. Nonetheless, Uschner seems to reflect on differences between German and Homer's Ionic Greek in a *distichon*, two lines of verse in which a pentameter follows a hexameter, redolent of *captatio benevolentiae*, a rhetorical technique to ensure goodwill:

> Deinen ionischen nahn germanische Laute mit Zagheit;
> Sei, Ermunterer, Du Deinem Ermunterten hold!
> (German sounds approach your Ionic ones timidly. You who encourage others, be charitable with the one you encouraged!)

1902 *Das alte Lied vom Zorne Achills (Urmenis)*, aus der *Ilias* ausgeschieden und metrisch übersetzt von August Fick, Göttingen.
Taylor Institution Library: 2931 e.46

The book is an attempt to identify the supposedly oldest parts of the *Iliad*, its 'primordial core' ('Urkern') according to certain numerical principles. By eliminating all the (allegedly) later additions to the text, thus shortening it to only 1936 verses, and by then translating these verses into German, Fick aims to make Homer accessible to school children. Fick's view is that the epic is too long to be enjoyed in its entirety:

> The *Iliad* [...] is composed of 15,639 verses! This begs the question how such an amount, which prevents any novel pleasure, could have come into being.
> (Die Ilias [...] besteht aus 15,693 Versen! Da fragt es sich, wie ein solcher allen frischen Genuß ausschließender Umfang entstanden sein kann.)

[1922] *Homers Ilias*, auf Grund der Übersetzungen von Johann Heinrich Voß verdeutscht von Hans Rupé, vol. 1: Erster bis zwölfter Gesang, Berlin/Leipzig.
Taylor Institution Library: REP.G.7250

3. Mapping Myth

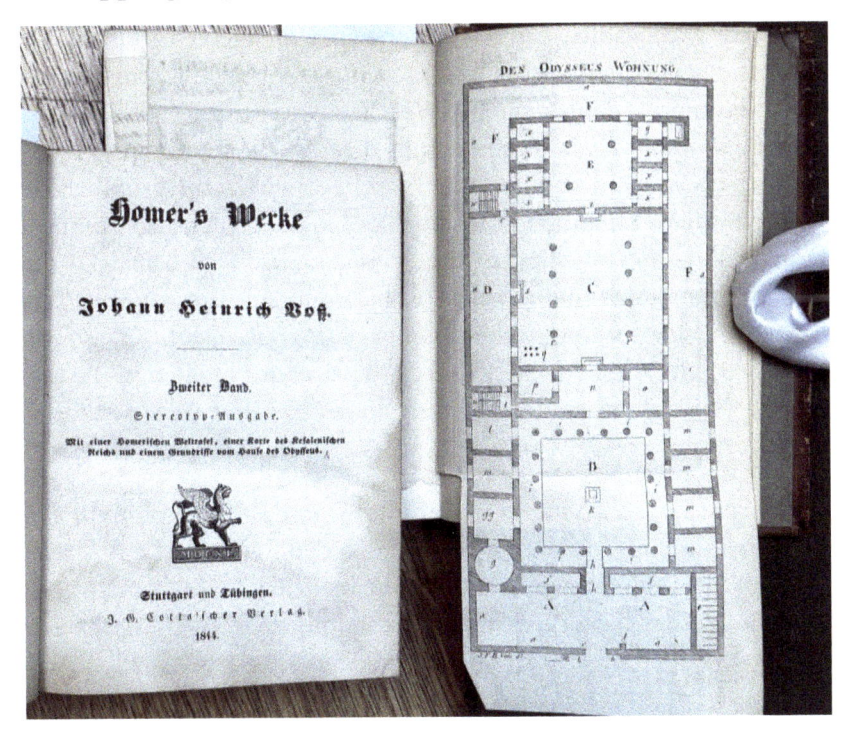

Illustration 14: The House of Odysseus (Voß 1844). Photograph: Philip Flacke

The Homeric epics and the *Nibelungenlied* each situate characters and action in a complex topography, mixing real place names and landmarks with imaginary and mythical spheres. This combination of historical events and characters with the ahistorical and the fantastic means that the narratives make it impossible to draw a line between fact and fiction. It may be precisely for this reason that locating the epics in the real world plays such an important role in the reception of both Homer and the *Nibelungenlied*. The tip of this iceberg could be the popular desire to discover the legendary treasure of the *Nibelungenhort* at the bottom of the Rhine, much like Schliemann in the 1870s when he claimed to have excavated Priam's Treasure. This was a major plot point in a 2023 episode of *Tatort* situated in Ludwigshafen am Rhein and entitled 'Gold'.

A number of maps and plans are included in an 1844 edition of Voss' *Iliad* and *Odyssey*, amongst them a plan of Odysseus' house in Ithaca complete with stables, kennel, and the spot for the vessels in which wine and water are mixed. The largest map shows the world according to Homer. It depicts the Mediterranean according to the outline shown on modern maps, but within this realistic topography it includes fictitious and mythical places and people like the cannibalistic Laestrygonians on an island in the Alboran Sea. A school edition of Franz Fühmann's retelling of the *Nibelungenlied* adds a map to the text that represents the 'Journey of the legendary Burgundians/Nibelungs [...] according to the account of the *Nibelungenlied* (around 1200 AD)'. Again, fictitious events and places are situated in the real world: '*Nibelungenhort* sunk in the Rhine', 'Etzel's castle: demise of the Nibelungs'. A German forest serves as backdrop.

A different way of trying to orient oneself in the world of myth can be seen in a copy of Gustav Schwab's retellings of Ancient Greek myth in the Taylorian collection. In the margins and on blank pages, a former reader has drawn numerous family trees of the gods and heroes described by Homer and his successors.

1844 *Homer's Werke* von Johann Heinrich Voß, Stereotyp-Ausgabe, erster Band, mit einer Karte von Troja, Stuttgart/Tübingen.
Taylor Institution Library: 52.A.1

1844 *Homer's Werke* von Johann Heinrich Voß, Stereotyp-Ausgabe, zweiter Band, mit einer Homerischen Welttafel, einer Karte des Kefalenischen Reichs und einem Grundrisse vom Hause des Odysseus, Stuttgart/Tübingen.
Taylor Institution Library: 52.A.1.A

1882 Gustav Schwab, *Die schönsten Sagen des klassischen Alterthums. Nach seinen Dichtern und Erzählern*, mit 8 Holzschnitten, 14th edition, Gütersloh/Leipzig.
Taylor Institution Library: MONTGOMERY.5.B.11

Section 3: Mapping Myth 61

Illustration 15: Section 3. From top to bottom, left to right:
Fry 2020, Mudrak 1955, Bartsch/de Boor 1988, Voß 1844, Fühmann 2005.
Photograph: Philip Flacke

62 Catalogue

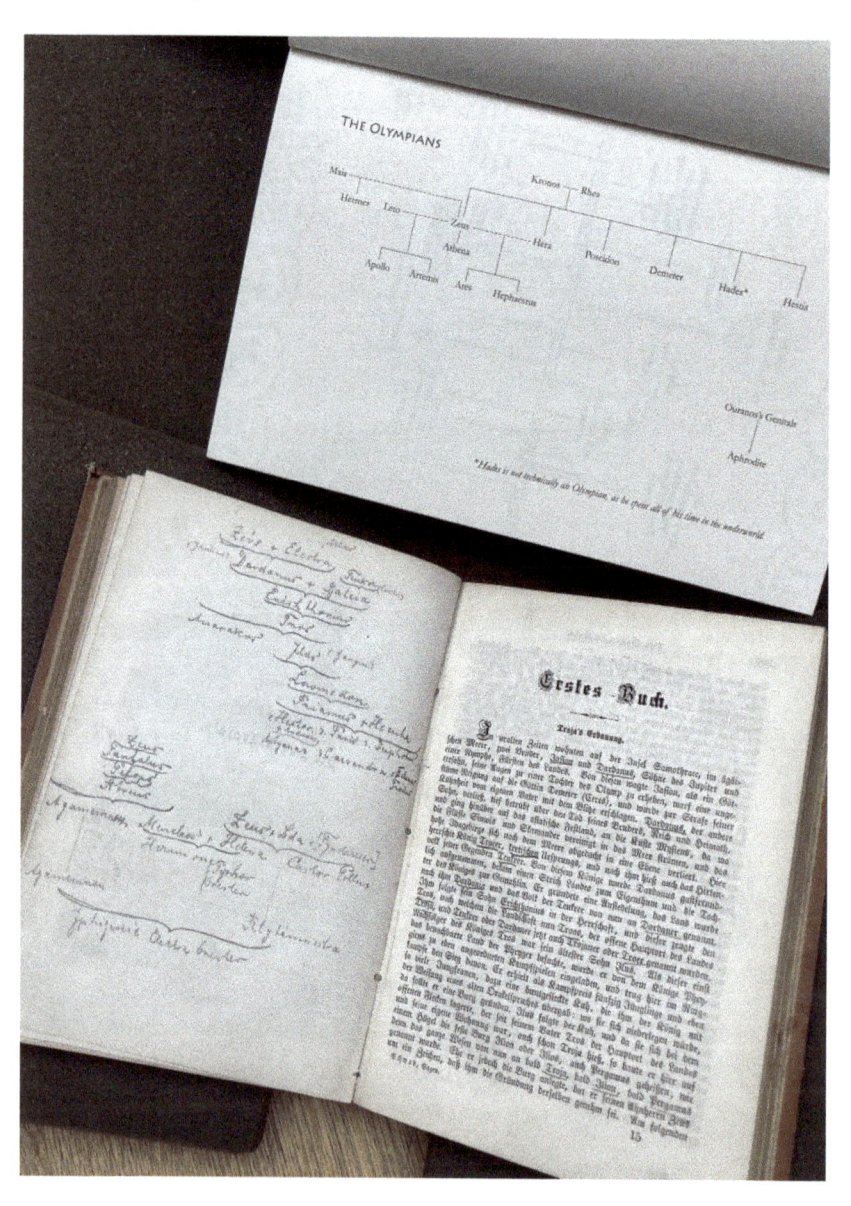

*Illustration 16: Section 3. Top: Fry 2020, bottom: Schwab 1882.
Photograph: Philip Flacke*

1955 *Deutsche Heldensagen*, herausgegeben von Edmund Mudrak, Reutlingen. Private loan

Mudrak, an Austrian ethnologist, filled various positions in Nazi Germany, gaining influence on both cultural and educational matters, and became professor at the University of Posen in occupied Poland in 1943. After the Second World War, Mudrak went on to publish a number of popular retellings of supposedly 'Germanic' myths, like this one, which builds on the popular book *Germanischer Sagenborn* (originally *Germania's Sagenborn* 1889/90) by the German author Emil Engelmann. Despite his political background, some of Mudrak's retellings are still in print.

1988 *Das Nibelungenlied*, nach der Ausgabe von Karl Bartsch herausgegeben von Helmut de Boor, 22. revidierte und von Roswitha Wisniewski ergänzte Auflage, Mannheim (Deutsche Klassiker des Mittelalters). Private loan

Helmut de Boor took over revising Bartsch's classic edition of the *Nibelungenlied* while being an active member of the Nazi Party, with the 10th edition coming out in 1940. He was dismissed from his position at the University of Bern in 1945 but took up the Chair at the Freie Universität Berlin, and became one of the most influential medievalists of post-war Germany.

1993 Franz Fühmann, *Der Nibelunge Not. Szenarium für einen Spielfilm*, mit einem Nachwort von Peter Göhler, Berlin.
Taylor Institution Library: SD.2682.A.1

2005 *Das Nibelungenlied*, neu erzählt von Franz Fühmann, mit Materialien, zusammengestellt von Isolde Schnabel, Stuttgart/Leipzig (Taschenbücherei Texte & Materialien). Private loan

2020 Stephen Fry, *Troy*, London.
Bodleian Library: XWeek 51 (20)

4. Powerful Women

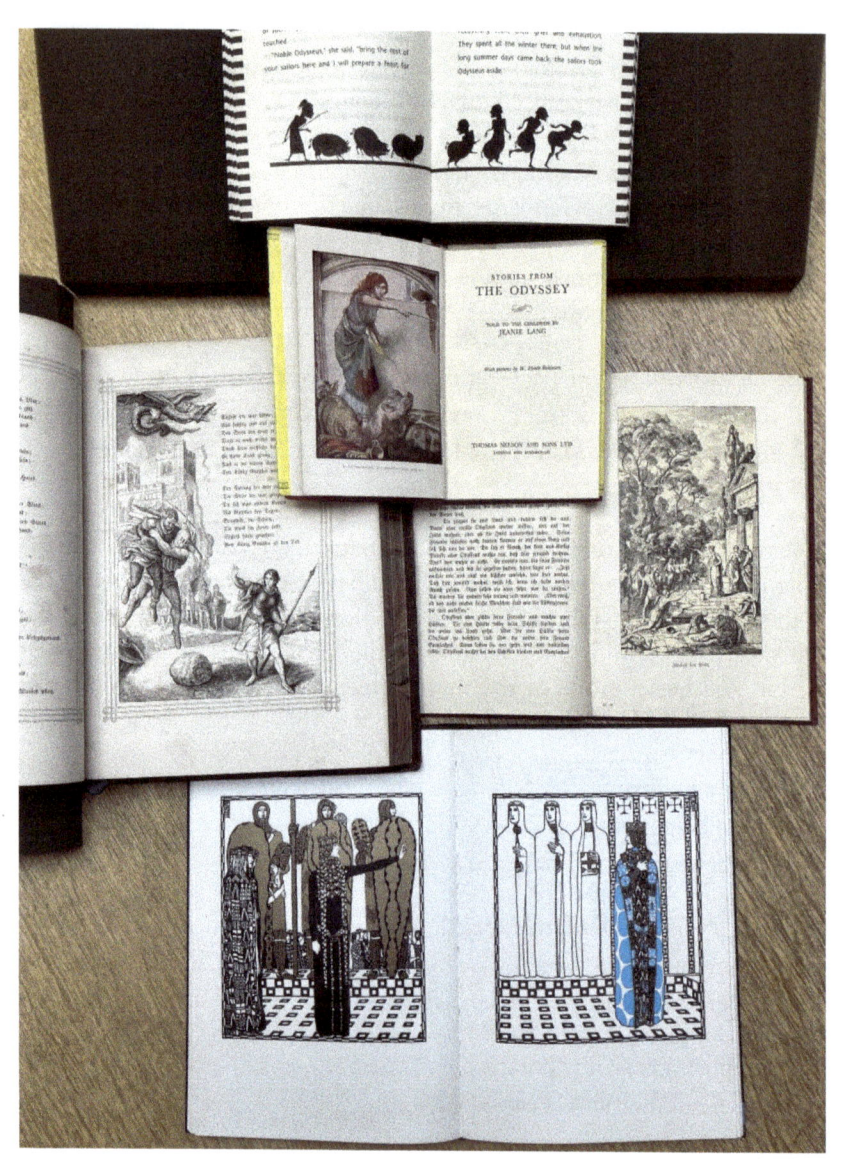

*Illustration 17: Section 4. From top to bottom, left to right:
Cross 2012, Lang n.d., Neureuther 1843, Otto 1903, Draesner 2016.
Photograph: Philip Flacke*

Section 4: Powerful Women 65

Illustration 18: Section 4. From top to bottom, left to right: Anon. 1907, Hoepke 1975, MacGregor 1908, Lamb 1926. Photograph: Philip Flacke

The stories of Homer and the *Nibelungenlied* have had a firm place in the canons of both adult and children's literature for generations.

This has meant a more or less constant demand for illustrated editions, popular retellings, and adaptations in simple language. While scholarly translations were historically done by men (the first women to translate the *Iliad* and the *Odyssey* into English being Caroline Alexander in 2015 and Emily Wilson in 2017 and 2023), women played an important part in adaptations for children.

Even if one excludes Homer's Olympian goddesses, who do not strictly have counterparts in the *Nibelungenlied*, various protagonists in all of these epics are both powerful and female. The illustrators depict them in various ways, sometimes with surprising similarities. There is surely some resemblance in the majestic postures and commanding gestures of both Circe and Brünhild, the one transforming Odysseus' men into pigs in a design by Friedrich Preller, reused for the 1903 edition of Helene Otto, the other ordering Kriemhild to stand still and stay behind in a design by Carl Otto Czeschka, reused in Ulrike Draesner's 2016 edition of the *Nibelungenlied*? Other illustrations differ in ways which tell us something about the underlying ideas of femininity and power. Are Brünhild and Circe depicted in their moments of superiority, or only when subdued by male heroes? Do they more resemble queens or witches? Are they sexualised and in what way?

1843 Gustav Pfizer, *Der Nibelungen Noth*, illustriert mit Holzschnitten nach Zeichnungen von Julius Schnorr von Carolsfeld und Eugen Neureuther, Stuttgart/Tübingen. Taylor Institution Library: 38.M.13

This verse translation of the *Nibelungenlied* into modern German had an enduring legacy because of its visual layout. It includes a large number of woodcuts produced by the Xylographische Anstalt von Kaspar Braun & [Georg] von Dessauer, based on illustrations by Julius Schnorr von Carolsfeld and Eugen Neureuther. Beginning in the 1820s, Schnorr created a series of frescoes to decorate the walls and ceilings of a series of rooms in the royal palace of King Ludwig I in Munich, and these had a second life as woodcuts. The woodcuts, as included by Pfizer, along with the related page design, found their way directly into a number of other *Nibelungenlied* translations, and were enormously influential for further *Nibelungenlied* translators and adapters.

1903 *Odyssee,* in der Sprache der Zehnjährigen erzählt von Helene Otto, mit 10 Vollbildern von Friedrich Preller und einer Vorrede an Eltern, Lehrer und Erzieher von B[erthold] Otto, Leipzig. Private loan

In the 'preface for parents, educators, and teachers', the German pedagogue Berthold Otto explains the educational value of, as the title says, a retelling of Homer 'in the language of ten-year-olds': Making sure children could actually understand what they were reading was meant to prevent an empty verbosity ('hohle Phrasenhaftigkeit') that they might otherwise acquire. The violence is not scaled down however which, when the story is told in childish words, has an unsettling effect – as for example in the punishment of the maids and the goatherd Melanthius: 'When everything was finished, they (Telemachus and the two herdsmen) brought the maids into the courtyard and hanged them all one after the other. Then they took Melanthius and cut off his nose and then his ears, and they broke his arms and legs so they were in pieces.' ('Als alles fertig war, führten sie (Telemach und die beiden Hirten) die Mägde in den Hof und hängten sie alle der Reihe nach auf. Dann nahmen sie den Melantheus und schnitten ihm die Nase und die Ohren ab und brachen ihm Arme und Beine kaputt.') The only omission is Melanthius' castration. (That his limbs are being broken instead of his hands and feet being cut off, is arguably a minor change.)

All the reader learns about the author of the book is that she was 'the teller of fairy tales and myths for her younger siblings and their playmates from earliest youth'. In fact, Helene Otto was Berthold's oldest daughter and only about 16 years when the book was published. (The text had already been published in her father's periodical 'Der Hauslehrer'.) In the course of one year after the publication of her *Odyssey,* there followed five retellings of canonical narratives by Helene Otto in the language of ten- or eight-year-olds, including two volumes on the Nibelungen myth and a version of the *Iliad.*

1907 Anonymous, *The Linden Leaf; or, The Story of Siegfried. Retold from the Nibelungen Lied,* London. Taylor Institution Library: 28849 f.4

This is another publication aimed at a young audience that includes eight brightly coloured illustrations, which seem to be signed 'Waugh'. It adapts the first half of the *Nibelungenlied,* also making brief reference to some other legends of Siegfried's youth. It ends after Siegfried's murder and, although it alludes to Kriemhild's desire to 'punish his murderer', there is no more explicit reference to her vengeance, and readers are assured that Hagen ultimately meets a hero's death, having 'fully atoned for his sins'.

1908 Mary MacGregor, *Stories of Siegfried, told to the children*, with pictures by Granville Fell, London/New York. Private loan

Unusually, this children's adaptation does not appeal to a shared Germanic heritage, but draws a distinction between 'the German hero', Siegfried, and 'your French and English heroes'. MacGregor draws on Norse material to an extent, but her primary source is the first half of the *Nibelungenlied*. She deals with the second half of the narrative in the final page, noting that Siegfried's death was eventually 'avenged by Queen Kriemhild', but implies that the violence was carried out only by men, and omits Kriemhild's own fate. There are eight colour plates by Granville Fell. The publication is undated, but 1908 is the usual date given. The exhibition features two other books from this series: *Stories from the Odyssey* and *Stories from the Iliad*.

[n.d.] Jeanie Lang, *Stories from the Odyssey, told to the children*, with pictures by W. Heath Robinson, London/Edinburgh. Private loan

This children's adaptation is part of the same 'Told to the children' series as *Stories of Siegfried* and *Stories from the Iliad*. The early-twentieth-century endeavour aimed to retell stories deemed to represent the western canon in language appropriate for 9-12 year-olds.

1926 Charles Lamb, *The Adventures of Ulysses*, with Illustrations by Doris Pailthorpe and T. H. Robinson, London et al.
Bodleian Library: 2527 e.819/20c

1975 *Homers Odyssee*, neu gefaßt von Hermann Hoepke mit 15 Linolschnitten von Hella Ackermann, Baden-Baden/Brüssel/Köln. Private loan

2012 Homer, *The Iliad and the Odyssey*, retold by Gillian Cross, with Illustrations by Neil Packer, London. Bodleian Library: XWeek 13 (18)

2016 Ulrike Draesner, *Nibelungen. Heimsuchung*, mit den Illustrationen von Carl Otto Czeschka, Stuttgart.
Taylor Institution Library: PT2664.R324 N53 DRA 2016

5. The Pierced Body

*Illustration 19: Section 5. From top to bottom, left to right:
Lang n.d., Otto 1904, Wägner/Heichen 1943, Cartwright 1907, Marbach 1840.
Photograph: Philip Flacke*

70   Catalogue

*Illustration 20: Section 5. From top to bottom, left to right:
Picard 1986, Hoepke 1977, Green 1974, Green 1965.
Photograph: Philip Flacke*

Blood springs forth in a high arch from the gaping wound of a dying Trojan. A spear is thrust through a man's neck. Siegfried sinks down looking at the weapon that protrudes from his chest. Simply put, these pictures – the majority of which appeared in children's books – spotlight violence. They showcase the severed body having been, or about to be, pierced by a weapon, and that weapon is always present. Two illustrations, by W. Heath Robinson and Betty Middleton-Sandford, do not actually depict stab wounds but show the dead lying beside the weapon that killed them. And yet everything appears to be clean. No dirt, no crusted blood stains the fabrics, spears, or shields; the plumed helmets look impeccable. How much do these pictures still inform our ideas of masculine heroism?

The stabbing of Siegfried was given ideological significance by right-wing German forces after the First World War. In a committee inquiring into the causes, prolongation, and loss of the war, the future Reichspräsident Paul von Hindenburg claimed to the German parliament that the German forces had been 'stabbed in the back'. With this historical lie, Hindenburg, who had himself been partly responsible for the military action, put the blame on democratic and socialist groups in Germany. These were claimed to have sabotaged the 'heroic' endeavours of the military. The 'Dolchstoßlegende' ('stab-in-the-back myth') was incorporated into right-wing narratives, quickly gaining antisemitic overtones, and was heavily used as propaganda by the Nazi party.

The *Nibelungenlied* made an abstract idea concrete in both text and image. Siegfried, who like Achilles can only be wounded on a single specific spot on his body, is murdered as he is lying down to drink from a spring. Hagen, vassal to his brother-in-law, stabs him from behind with his own spear. Hindenburg and others were ready to cast the German forces in the role of Siegfried, an almost invulnerable hero who could only have been brought down by treacherous deceit. In the course of this, the spear of the *Nibelungenlied* became the prototypical backstabbing weapon: a dagger (the 'Dolch' part of the 'Dolchstoß'). The image of the 'Dolchstoß' served as an essential component in the project of linking the *Nibelungen* to national identity. This is emphasised in a 1943 edition of *Germanic Tales about Gods and Heroes* (*Germanische Götter- und Heldensagen*), which shows a still from Fritz Lang's two-part film series *Die Nibelungen* (1924) as its frontispiece.

1840 *Das Nibelungenlied*. Uebersetzt von Gotthard Oswald Marbach, mit Holzschnitten nach Originalzeichnungen von Eduard Bendemann und Julius Hübner, Denkmal zur vierten Säcularfeier der Buchdruckerkunst, Leipzig. Private loan

Gotthard Oswald Marbach was Richard Wagner's brother-in-law and an associate professor at the University of Leipzig. Beginning in 1838, he issued a sprawling series of *Volksbücher* over a relatively short number of years, often intervening dramatically in the material – though he appears to have been relatively careful with the *Nibelungenlied*. Other German translators of medieval literature, in particular Karl Simrock, held Marbach in low regard. As a work of *Druckkunst*, the art of printing, however, this book was a dramatic statement of what could be accomplished in the interaction of text and image.

1904 *Ilias*, in der Sprache der Zehnjährigen erzählt von Helene Otto, mit 6 Vollbildern von C[arl] Bertling, Leipzig. Private loan

Helene Otto's *Iliad* claims the same naturalistic authenticity as her *Odyssey* a year earlier. 'Of course, you all know that you're not supposed to write like this in an essay. But here everything is written down and printed as it is actually spoken.' ('Ihr wißt natürlich alle, daß man so im Aufsatz nicht schreiben darf. Aber hier ist alles so aufgeschrieben und gedruckt, wie es wirklich gesprochen wird.') So goes a footnote explaining why the preposition *wegen* is colloquially used with dative instead of genitive. Again, the child-like language contrasts sharply with the violent action – as in the description of the scene depicted here (cf. *Il.* 11, 451–479). The recurring phrase *totmachen* for 'kill' is hard to translate. Literally meaning 'to make dead', it lends the register of the very young to a brutal action.

> At last, he also struck dead a very brave Trojan. Then his brother came. He said to Odysseus: 'Either you are dead or I am dead.' At once, he threw his lance at him. The lance went through the shield

Section 5: The Pierced Body

and through the armour and cut Odysseus' skin. Then, Pallas Athena stopped the lance so that the lance wouldn't kill Odysseus. Odysseus realised that he wasn't wounded so very badly that he would die. Then, he threw his lance after the one who had wounded him, and he struck him between his shoulders because he had wanted to run away and had turned round.

(Zuletzt schlug er auch noch einen sehr tapferen Troer tot. Da kam dem sein Bruder. Der sagte zu Odysseus: 'Entweder du machst mich tot, oder ich mach dich tot.' Dabei warf er nach ihm mit der Lanze. Die Lanze ging durch den Schild durch und durch den Panzer durch und ritzte dem Odysseus die Haut. Dann hielt Pallas Athene die Lanze auf, damit die Lanze den Odysseus nicht tot machte. Odysseus merkte, daß er noch nicht so sehr schlimm verwundet war, daß er sterben mußte. Er warf nun seine Lanze nach dem, der ihn verwundet hatte, und er traf ihn zwischen die Schultern, denn der hatte ausreißen wollen und hatte sich dazu umgedreht.)

According to inscriptions on the front endpapers, both copies of Otto's Homer retellings shown in the exhibition used to belong to a book collection owned by the 'Elternbund der deutschen Erneuerungsgemeinde'. Founded in 1904, the 'Deutsche Erneuerungs-Gemeinde' ('German community for renewal') aimed to establish settlements in rural Brandenburg built on ideas of racial purity and Germanic 'land-right', an antisemitic world view, and anti-modern resentment.

[n.d.] Jeanie Lang, *Stories from the Iliad; or, The Siege of Troy, told to the children*, with pictures by W. Heath Robinson, London/New York.
Private loan

This children's adaptation is part of the same 'Told to the children' series as *Stories of Siegfried* and *Stories from the Odyssey* (above). This was an early-twentieth-century endeavour which aimed to retell stories deemed to represent the western canon in language appropriate for 9-12 year-olds.

1907 Tho[ma]s Cartwright, *Sigurd the Dragon-Slayer. A Twice-Told Tale*, London (Every Child's Library).
Bodleian Library: 930 f.107

Cartwright offers a retelling for children, first of the Norse material 'as fashioned ... for the delight of our sea-roving Viking forefathers', and then of the *Nibelungenlied*, 'for which we are indebted to our cousins, the Germans'. The text of the latter section is taken entirely from Thomas Carlyle. In addition to eight colour plates, there are numerous black and white engravings. No details are given for the illustrator(s), but some of the black and white images are accompanied by the monogram 'I.B.'. It does not appear that on this occasion Cartwright worked with Patten Wilson, who illustrated his *Brave Beowulf* in the same series. In a preamble intended to appear handwritten, Cartwright invokes William Morris's comparison of the *Nibelungen* material to the Homeric epics.

1943 *Walhalla. Germanische Götter- und Heldensagen*, nach den hochdeutschen Fassungen von Simrock und Wägner bearbeitet von Walter Heichen, Berlin. Private loan

1965 *The Tale of Troy*, retold from the Ancient authors by Roger Lancelyn Green, illustrated by Betty Middleton-Sandford, London. Private loan

1974 *The Tale of Troy*, retold from the Ancient authors by Roger Lancelyn Green, illustrated by Pauline Baynes, London. Private loan

1977 *Homers Ilias*, neugefaßt von Hermann Hoepke mit 13 Holzschnitten von Hella Ackermann, Baden-Baden/Köln/New York. Private loan

1986 *The Iliad & Odyssey of Homer*, retold for children by Barbara Leonie Picard, illustrated by Joan Kiddel-Monroe, Oxford (The Oxford Children's Classics). Bodleian Library: 25398 e.3747

6. Violent Revenge

*Illustration 21: Section 6. From top to bottom, left to right:
Church 1907, Mackenzie 1912, Hands 1880,
Agrimbau/Klassen 2018 (Odyssey), Colum 1920, Atwood 2018.
Photograph: Philip Flacke*

76 Catalogue

*Illustration 22: Section 6. From top to bottom, left to right:
Church 1908, Anon. 1911, Agrimbau/Klassen 2018 (Iliad), Hands 1880,
Miller 2011, Picard 1986 (for the last see section 5).
Photograph: Philip Flacke*

Section 6: Violent Revenge 77

Both the *Odyssey* and the *Nibelungenlied* end in bloodbath: The disguised Odysseus, coming home to his wife Penelope and his son Telemachus twenty years after he set off for Troy, finds his house full of suitors who eat and drink at his expense and want to marry his supposed widow. He finally traps them in his hall and kills them all with the help of Telemachus and two herdsmen. Twelve maids, whom Odysseus believes to have been disloyal to him, are forced to clean up the blood of the suitors and are then hanged on Odysseus' command. Margaret Atwood in her 2005 novella *The Penelopiad* gives the twelve maids the role of a Greek choir, giving them the chance to speak for themselves and comment on events.

Like Odysseus, Kriemhild orders the slaughter of those upon whom she wants to take vengeance. At her invitation, the Burgundians, whom she holds responsible for the death of her first husband Siegfried, come to the castle of her second husband, Etzel. There, they are all killed in the feasting hall. The slaughter of the suitors and the slaughter of the Burgundians are depicted in ways that share some similar features. For one, the heroes appear above a pile of corpses. But where do the similarities end? With whom is the viewer supposed to sympathise, if at all? Is the violence imagined as just? Is it glorified or abhorred, downplayed or celebrated?

Kriemhild herself takes part in the violence, transgressing both medieval and Victorian gender roles. At one point, she appears before Hagen holding the decapitated head of her brother and his former king. She will imminently go on to decapitate another man, this time with her own hands, and it will be Hagen. This scene often features in illustration, including in Lydia Hands' *Nibelungenlied* adaptation 'for the use of young readers', which reuses the designs by Julius Schnorr von Carolsfeld and Eugen Neureuther, mediated through their slightly revised appearance in one of Karl Simrock's *Nibelungenlied* translations. Children's versions of the *Iliad*, too, sometimes depict the mutilated dead body – or rather, the public desecration of a corpse that by divine intervention cannot be mutilated. In Helene Otto's *Odyssey* for ten-year-olds, Achilles can be seen on a chariot dragging Hector's corpse around the walls of Troy to avenge the death of his lover Patroclus. Madeline Miller's 2011 novel *The Song of Achilles* tells the story of Achilles and Patroclus as a queer reading of the *Iliad*.

1880 Lydia Hands, *Golden Threads from an Ancient Loom. Das Nibelunglied*, adapted to the use of young readers, with fourteen wood engravings by Julius Schnorr, of Carolsfeld, London/New York. Private loan

Golden Threads is the first of the flood of children's adaptations of *Nibelungen*-related material in the later nineteenth and early twentieth centuries. It is unusually complete amongst works aimed at children in adapting the full narrative, albeit with some obfuscation. The narrative was augmented with additional legends of Siegfried, all found in Thomas Carlyle's essay, and Carlyle was the dedicatee. The woodcuts and the corresponding layout are a selection from those which originally appeared in Pfizer's *Der Nibelungen Noth* (1843), though Hands discovered them in, and reproduced them from, a translation by Karl Simrock, published in 1873. She casts Kriemhild as driven to violence by madness – an excuse for violent women also used in legal contexts.

1897 Margaret Armour, *The Fall of the Nibelungs*, illustrated and decorated by W.B. MacDougall, London.
Taylor Institution Library: FIEDLER.G.600

Armour's *Fall of the Nibelungs* is relatively unusual amongst complete translations of the *Nibelungenlied* into English in being illustrated – and her illustrator was her husband. It was more common for illustrations to appear in adaptations. Translators were often overtly concerned to present their work as scholarly, and this was often taken to preclude images. Armour intended her translation to be a close rendering of the medieval text in modern English prose, and it was well received as such. Like most nineteenth-century anglophone translators, however, she also made use of a modern German translation, in this case a parallel text edition by Karl Simrock, which offered access to the Middle High German alongside a modern German text.

1907 *The Children's Odyssey*, told from Homer in simple language by Alfred J. Church, with twelve ills, London. Bodleian Library: 2932 e.39

Section 6: Violent Revenge

1908 *The Children's Iliad*., told from Homer in simple language by Alfred J. Church, with twelve illustrations, London.
Bodleian Library: 2931 e.52

1911 Anonymous, *Siegfried and Kriemhild. A Story of Passion and Revenge*, illustrated by Frank C. Papé, London et al. (The World's Romances).
Bodleian Library: 28849 d.25

This is a relatively thorough retelling of the *Nibelungenlied* for children, with the framing device that it is told in a tavern in Worms in 1460. The Kriemhild of this adaptation is ultimately even more violent than the medieval Kriemhild, killing her brother, as well as Hagen, herself, but the author follows Lydia Hands in implying that her actions are the result of madness. The text is accompanied by eight colour plates by Frank Cheyne Papé (1878–1972).

1912 Donald Mackenzie, *Teutonic Myths and Legend. An Introduction to the Edday & Sagas, Beowulf, The Nibelungenlied, etc.*, London.
Bodleian Library: 930 e.541

Mackenzie's collection of shortened retellings described itself as 'an introduction to the *Eddas* and Sagas, *Beowulf*, The *Nibelungenlied*. etc.'. It was aimed at adults and, like other similar publications, included a number of images previously published elsewhere. The image displayed is based on one of Julius Schnorr von Carolsfeld's frescoes – and notably not a woodcut version. The publication is undated, but 1912 is the usual date given.

1920 Padraic Colum, *The Adventures of Odysseus and the Tale of Troy*, presented [=illustrated] by Willy Pogány, London.
Bodleian Library: 2932 e.53

2011 Madeline Miller, *The Song of Achilles*, London et al.
Bodleian Library: XWeek 36 (11)

2018 Diego Agrimbau and Smilton Roa Klassen, *Homer's The Iliad. A Graphic Novel*, Oxford. Bodleian Library: XWeek 35 (17)

2018 Diego Agrimbau and Smilton Roa Klassen, *Homer's The Odyssey. A Graphic Novel*, Oxford. Bodleian Library: XWeek 35 (17)

2018 Margaret Atwood, *The Penelopiad*, Edinburgh (Canons/The Myths). Private loan

2020 Playmobil 70469 – *Achilles and Patroclus with Chariot*, plastic toy figures, Zirndorf. Private loan

The toy figures of Achilles and Patroclus, sold by a company in Bavaria, are part of a series with sets of different characters from Greek myth. According to the manufacturer, they are aimed at four- to ten-year-olds. On the Playmobil website, Achilles and Patroclus are introduced not as lovers but as 'friends since childhood', always standing 'side by side in battle'. Children are then encouraged to reenact Patroclus' death and Achilles avenging him in his battle against Hector – notwithstanding Hector not being included in the set: 'But one day Patroclus puts on Achilles' armour and rides into battle alone. There he is killed by Hector, the prince of Troy, who mistakenly believes him to be Achilles. Achilles is furious about the death of his friend and sets out to avenge him and kill Hector.' Although Playmobil has produced toy versions of a number of men who serve as key figures in German national identity – Dürer, Luther, Bach, Goethe, Schiller –, there are no sets based on the *Nibelungenlied*.

Section 6: *Violent Revenge*   81

Illustration 23: Playmobil set for section 6. In the background, left to right: Lang n.d. (section 5), Colum 1920 (section 6), Church 1908 (section 6); under the horses: Green 1965 (section 5).
Photograph: Philip Flacke

Bodleian Library: Homeric Fragments curated by NIGEL WILSON and PETER TÓTH

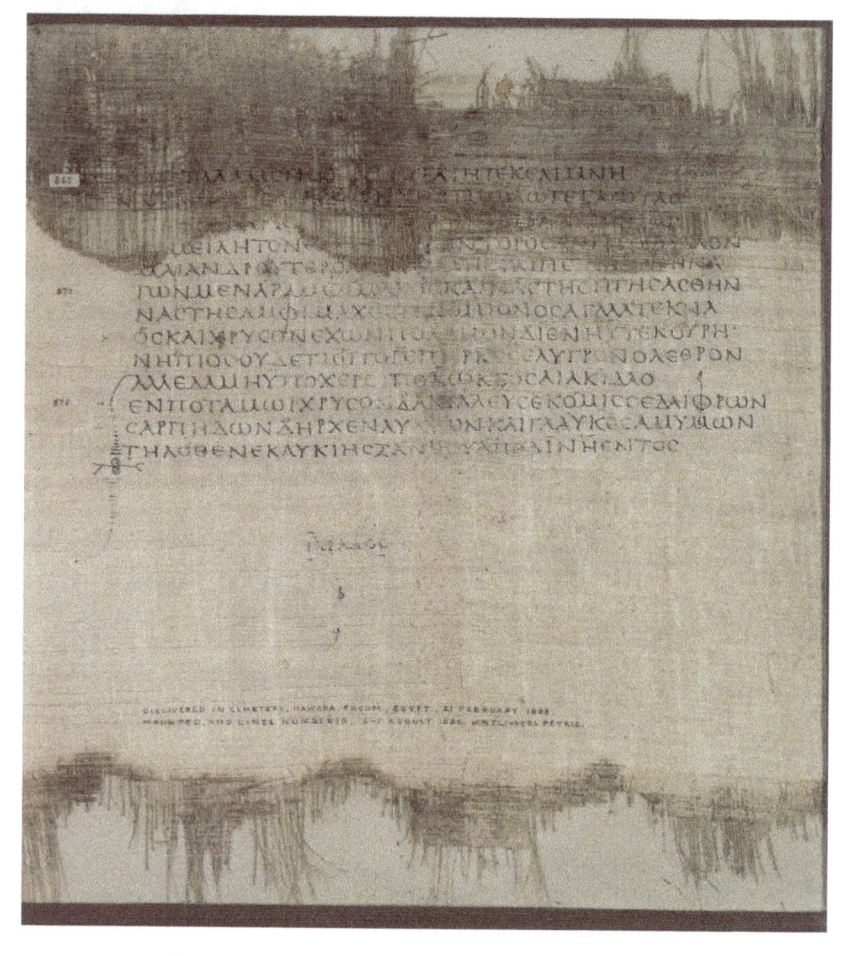

Illustration 24: The Hawara Homer. End of Book 2

Homeric Fragments

1. Bodleian Library, MS. Gr. class. a. 1(P)/1-10 = p. Hawara (c. 150), papyrus.
   https://medieval.bodleian.ox.ac.uk/catalog/manuscript_4977

This papyrus, the 'Hawara Homer', dating from the second century A.D., contains part of *Iliad* Book 2. It is noteworthy for the use of marginal signs invented by Alexandrian scholars to indicate lines that should be deleted or were thought to raise other points of interest.

2. Bodleian Library, MS. Auct. V. 1. 51. (late 10th cent.), parchment.
   https://medieval.bodleian.ox.ac.uk/catalog/manuscript_874

The Homeric poems retained their place in the school curriculum, but linguistic changes posed an increasingly difficult problem for the pupils. This MS, probably written at the turn of the tenth and eleventh centuries, is a glossary for readers of the *Odyssey*. It is far from certain that the average pupil could afford such a book, and this one probably belonged to a relatively well-off schoolmaster.

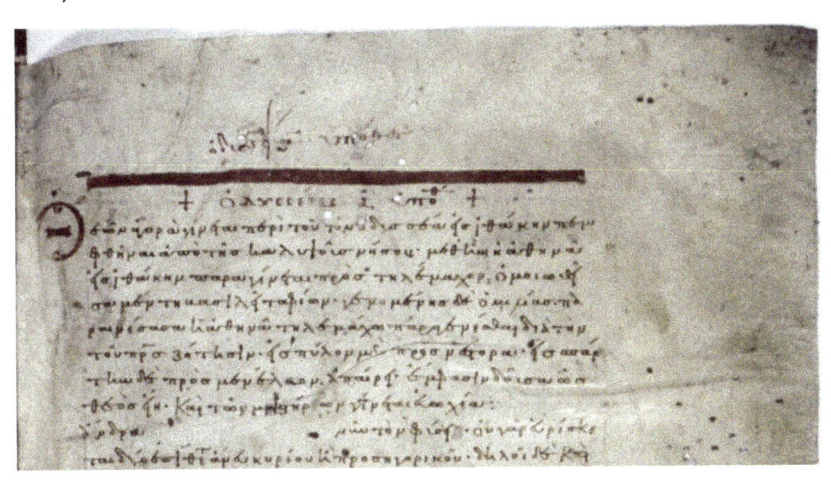

Illustration 25: Bodleian Library, MS. Auct. V. 1. 51., fol. 1r. The text shown here is a synopsis of Book 1 of the Odyssey

3. Bodleian Library, MS. Auct. T. 2. 7 (12th cent.), parchment.
https://medieval.bodleian.ox.ac.uk/catalog/manuscript_784

A copy of the *Iliad*, probably from the early twelfth century, with extensive marginalia, mostly paraphrase. The script is rather cursive.

4. Bodleian Library, MS. Laud gr. 54 (early 15th cent.), paper.
https://medieval.bodleian.ox.ac.uk/catalog/manuscript_6866

This copy of the *Iliad* from the early fifteenth century contains Books 1-2 only. The limited content could be regarded as a sign of drastic reduction of the curriculum, of which there is other evidence.

5. Bodleian Library, MS. Canonici gr. 43 (16th cent.), paper.
https://medieval.bodleian.ox.ac.uk/catalog/manuscript_2477

This is a 16th-century copy of *Iliad* Books 1-10. Though the text had been printed in Florence in 1488 and by Aldus in 1504 hand-written copies continued to be produced.

5. Bodleian Library, MS. Canonici gr. 79 (early 16th cent.), paper.
https://medieval.bodleian.ox.ac.uk/catalog/manuscript_2509

Ilias Latina (Epitome Iliadis)

6. Bodleian Library, Auct. F. 2.14, fol. 90r (12th cent.), parchment.
https://medieval.bodleian.ox.ac.uk/catalog/manuscript_610

This miscellany includes the *Ilias Latina*. It was probably produced in the second half of the twelfth century, perhaps at Winchester or Sherborne.

7. Bodleian Library, MS. Rawlinson G. 57 (12th cent.), parchment.
https://medieval.bodleian.ox.ac.uk/catalog/manuscript_8593

Another twelfth-century miscellany containing the *Ilias Latina*.

Illustration 26: 'myths retold' display at Blackwell's Bookshop, Broad Street Oxford, in May 2024. Photograph: Philip Flacke

Treasures of the Taylorian:
Series Three: Cultural Memory
Volume 7

Mary Boyle, Philip Flacke,
Timothy Powell

Epic!

Homer and the *Nibelungenlied* in Translation

Editor: Henrike Lähnemann

Taylor Institution Library, Oxford, 2024

TAYLOR INSTITUTION LIBRARY

TAYLOR INSTITUTION LIBRARY
St Giles, Oxford, OX1 3NA

https://www.bodleian.ox.ac.uk/libraries/taylor/exhibitions-and-publications

© 2024 The Authors

Some rights are reserved. This book is made available under the Creative Commons Attribution-Non-Commercial-No Derivative Works 4.0 International (CC BY 4.0). This license allows for copying any part of the work for personal and non-commercial use, providing author attribution is clearly stated.

Digital downloads for this volume are available at https://historyofthebook.mml.ox.ac.uk/epic-homer-and-nibelungenlied-in-translation/
They include a pdf ebook of the text
and an expanded exhibition catalogue.

The cover image features the woodcut illustration for the first 'Abenteuer' of *Das Nibelungenlied* in the translation by Gotthard Oswald Marbach based on a drawing by Julius Hübner, published as monument for the centenary celebration for printing, *Denkmal zur vierten Säcularfeier der Buchdruckerkunst*, Leipzig 1840.

Catalogue accompanying the exhibition 'Epic! Homer and the *Nibelungenlied* in Translation' in the Voltaire Room of the Taylor Institution Library, Oxford 22 May to 13 June 2024.

Typesetting by Henrike Lähnemann
Cover design by Emma Huber

ISBN 978-1-8384641-8-9

Printed in the United Kingdom and United States by Lightning Source for Taylor Institution Library

Table of Contents

HENRIKE LÄHNEMANN – Preface	v
JOHN BUTCHER – Introduction	vii
PHILIP FLACKE – The *Nibelungenlied* as 'German *Iliad*'	1
Appendix: 'A German *Iliad*'. Endorsements and Critique	5
MARY BOYLE – The Victorian *Nibelungenlied*	14
Epic Adaptations for Children	20
TIMOTHY POWELL – The *Nibelungenlied* from National Socialist Epic to Socialist National Epic	24
Appendix: Epic Beginnings	
Iliad	40
Odyssey	44
Nibelungenlied	47

Exhibition Catalogue

Taylorian: Epic! Homer and the *Nibelungenlied* in Translation
curated by MARY BOYLE and PHILIP FLACKE

Section 1: Epic?	50
Section 2: Translating Epic Verse	55
Section 3: Mapping Myth	59
Section 4: Powerful Women	64
Section 5: The Pierced Body	69
Section 6: Violent Revenge	75

Bodleian Library: Homeric Fragments
curated by NIGEL WILSON and PETER TÓTH   82

Illustration 1: The statues above the entrance to the Taylorian representing languages taught in Oxford in the 19th century. Photograph: Henrike Lähnemann

Henrike Lähnemann
Preface

The exhibition 'Epic! Homer and the *Nibelungenlied* in Translation' accompanies the workshop 'The Reading and Reception of the Homeric Poems and the *Nibelungenlied* in Germany and Europe from the Eighteenth Century to the Present'. Both build on one of the founding principles of the Taylor Institution Library: to chart the development of 'Nationalliteratur' in the context of 'Weltliteratur'. The four figures standing proud over the St Giles entrance of the building represent French, German, Italian, and Spanish literature as a group of women, collectively fighting, scattering a cornucopia, enlightening, and, last but not least, thinking. The library itself was founded in the 19th century, at the time of establishing the 'canon' of German literature, dedicated to making texts in their original form available to students, starting with incunables and going to the newest contemporary literature.

This book and exhibition stand at the intersection of two larger projects: that of the year-long celebration of the legacy of the *Nibelungenlied* by the Meran Academy (more on that later by its organiser John Butcher); and that of the 'Cultural Memory' series of the 'Treasures of the Taylorian'. The latter is dedicated to uncovering hidden connections between collections of the Taylorian and wider topics and issues, for example between the Reformation pamphlets held by the library and Expressionist art (volume 5), or between book layout and multilingual writing (volume 2).

In 2022, Mary Boyle organised an exhibition 'Violent Victorian Medievalism' which turned into volume 4 of the series. Her essay focussing on the representation of women, heroes and violence in English *Nibelungenlied* adaptations has been combined with her discussion of how to translate violence for children into one of the three introductory essays of this book.

The new introductory essay by Philip Flacke discusses the trope of the 'German *Iliad*' which is so ubiquitous that we have dedicated one of the appendices to a survey of its appearance in literature. It starts with the first editions of both the Homeric and medieval epic texts and their inculturation into a history of the German nation – something that all subsequent adaptations have to grapple with. This is particularly striking in the third essay by Timothy Powell who highlights how the GDR appropriated (with difficulties!) the *Nibelungenlied* which had been tainted by National Socialism. Taken together, the three essays follow the stages of (re-)discovery of the *Nibelungenlied* from the 18th century, focussing on the aspect of reading it as national epos and, to this end, linking it with longer established icons of epic literature, most prominently Homer's *Iliad* and *Odyssey*.

The centre of the book is the exhibition catalogue which combines precious first editions of translations of the 18th and 19th centuries with cheap popular adaptations particularly for children. The exhibition builds on the Taylorian collection, supplemented from Bodleian holdings and private loans from the organisers – it took us all by surprise how much relevant epic material was amongst the formative books on our shelves!

We are grateful to all who helped make this exhibition and catalogue happen: Emma Huber, the librarians and interns at the Taylorian; Thomas Wood and other helpful proofreaders in Oxford and beyond; all contributors to the workshop 'The Reading and Reception of the Homeric Poems and the *Nibelungenlied* in Germany and Europe from the Eighteenth Century to the Present'; above all for the initiative and the support to the Meran Academy, particularly John Butcher, who coordinated the European-wide project – now more important than ever!

Oxford, 15 May 2024
Henrike Lähnemann for the organisers and authors

*Illustration 2: The poster by the Meran Academy for the event.
Design: Meran Academy*

JOHN BUTCHER
Introduction

The Meran Academy, founded in 1949 and celebrating this year its seventy-fifth anniversary, is a non-profit association whose goal is to foster cultural and scientific ties between the German- and Italian-speaking areas. In the past decade, its research and educational projects have been focused to a considerable degree on the European reception of literary classics such as Dante's *Commedia*, Ariosto's *Orlando Furioso* and Tasso's *Gerusalemme Liberata*. Its most recent initiative switches to a classic of German poetry, the anonymous medieval epic entitled *Nibelungenlied*, circulating widely from somewhere around 1200 onwards.

Taking its cue from a *Nibelungenlied* manuscript once housed in Obermontani Castle in the nearby town of Latsch (Vinschgau), the multilingual research and educational project *"Da brachte man die Märe in andrer Könge Land". Europäische Überlieferung und Strahlkraft des* Nibelungenliedes */ La fortuna europea del* Cantare dei Nibelunghi, coordinated by Verena Pohl alongside Federica Gazzani, provides a wide-ranging series of conferences and lectures within the Meran Academy. Further events taking place in South Tyrol, Italy and England, hosted by partner institutions, aim to widen the scope of the project, exploring lesser-known facets of the reception of the *Nibelungenlied*.

An initial conference in Meran investigated the manuscript tradition of the *Nibelungenlied*, including an analysis of the variants of the Obermontani manuscript (ms. I) compared to the text of Codex Sangallensis 857 (ms. B), as well as a discussion of the Ambraser Heldenbuch (ms. d), produced in South Tyrol by Hans Ried from Bozen by order of Emperor Maximilian I himself. A second conference in Marienberg Abbey, on the western border of South Tyrol's meandering Vinschgau, delved into the complex personality of Beda Weber, that Benedictine monk and scholar who in 1834 discovered in Obermontani Castle, buried beneath rags and other rubbish, the parchment ms. I of the *Nibelungenlied*: he acquired the priceless artefact for the princely sum of 10 florins, today the equivalent of a few hundred pounds. A third conference in South Tyrol's capital Bozen, planned by the local Società Dante Alighieri, compared and contrasted the two poetic masterpieces of the Italian and German Middle Ages, the *Divine Comedy* and the *Nibelungenlied*, highlighting similarities and differences in the portrayal of specific characters; extracts from Dante's poem and the *Nibelungenlied* were read in the original Italian and Middle High German by Marta Penchini and myself. A fourth conference took place in the magnificent setting of Villa Vigoni on Lake Como and revolved around the arrival of the Nibelungs in Italy: the first event of its sort ever to take place, it opened with a paper by the pioneer in the field, Verio Santoro, and moved freely from Giosue Carducci's verses to Italian parodies of Wagner's tetralogy and comics.

Illustration 3: Meran Academy. Photograph: Meran Academy

Forthcoming events comprise a large-scale conference on the European reception of the medieval poem, due to be held at the Academy, with papers on Denmark, Holland, Hungary, Ukraine, the United Kingdom, Greece and other nations: a paper on France, for example, will survey Ernest Reyer's *Sigurd* (1884), a hybrid opera mixing the *Nibelungenlied* and Wagner's *Ring des Nibelungen*, and Hélène Cixous' subtle and profoundly poetic tragedy *L'Histoire (qu'on ne connaîtra jamais)* (1994). A final conference will be meeting further afield in Trieste and setting out to consider the theory of diachronic translation by way of the *Nibelungenlied*: amongst other features, it will have the honour of presenting the first Slovenian translation of the German epic, composed by Simon Širca.

The research and educational project at the Meran Academy *"Da brachte man die Märe in andrer Könge Land". Europäische Überlieferung und Strahlkraft des* Nibelungenliedes */ La fortuna europea del* Cantare dei Nibelunghi, also including school visits throughout South Tyrol, individual history lectures, book presentations, a cultural evening in Latsch and the four-part lecture series *Das* Nibelungenlied *und…*, forms part of a considerably larger initiative, NIBELUNGEN. Die Rückkehr. Il ritorno, organised in association with Kunst Meran and its dynamic director Martina Oberprantacher. The latter institution is currently playing host to an exhibition curated by Harald F. Theiss: *Imagine Worlds*. The centrepiece of this exhibition is the Obermontani manuscript, which Berlin's Staatsbibliothek has most kindly lent for the occasion, thus allowing it to return to that Alpine region in whose castles it was preserved for at least three and a half centuries (c. 1472–1834).

The Reading and Reception of the Homeric Poems and the Nibelungenlied *in Germany and Europe from the Eighteenth Century to the Present* constitutes an integral part of the Meran project. I am grateful to Nigel Wilson for having broadened the initiative to the University of Oxford and to Henrike Lähnemann for having guided the event into the exceptionally rich and multi-faceted programme of Oxford Medieval Studies.

Gargazon (South Tyrol), 5 May 2024,
John Butcher

Illustration 4: Obermontani castle. Photograph: John Butcher

Obermontani Castle is located above the town of Latsch in the lower Vinschgau (South Tyrol), at the entrance to the Martelltal. It was built by Albert of Tyrol in 1228 in order to counterbalance the weight of the Diocese of Chur. From 1300 onwards, it belonged to the lords of Montani, who during the Fifteenth century significantly enlarged the premises. Later, as the lords of Montani became extinct, the castle passed into the hands of the counts of Mohr who presumably stored there the renowned library once owned by the local intellectual Anton von Annenberg (1427/1428-1483) and consisting of around 250 volumes. In 1833, after the death of the last of the Mohrs, the castle fell rapidly into disrepair and its marbles were plundered by greedy farmers. All that remains today is a ruin currently closed to the public. There is good reason to believe that ms. I of the *Nibelungenlied* was kept in one of the rooms of the palas (residential quarters) and that Beda Weber unearthed it there in 1834. The somewhat spartan interior, without any traces of previous mural paintings, is offset by impressive brickwork and windows providing stunning views over the Alpine landscape of the Vinschgau.

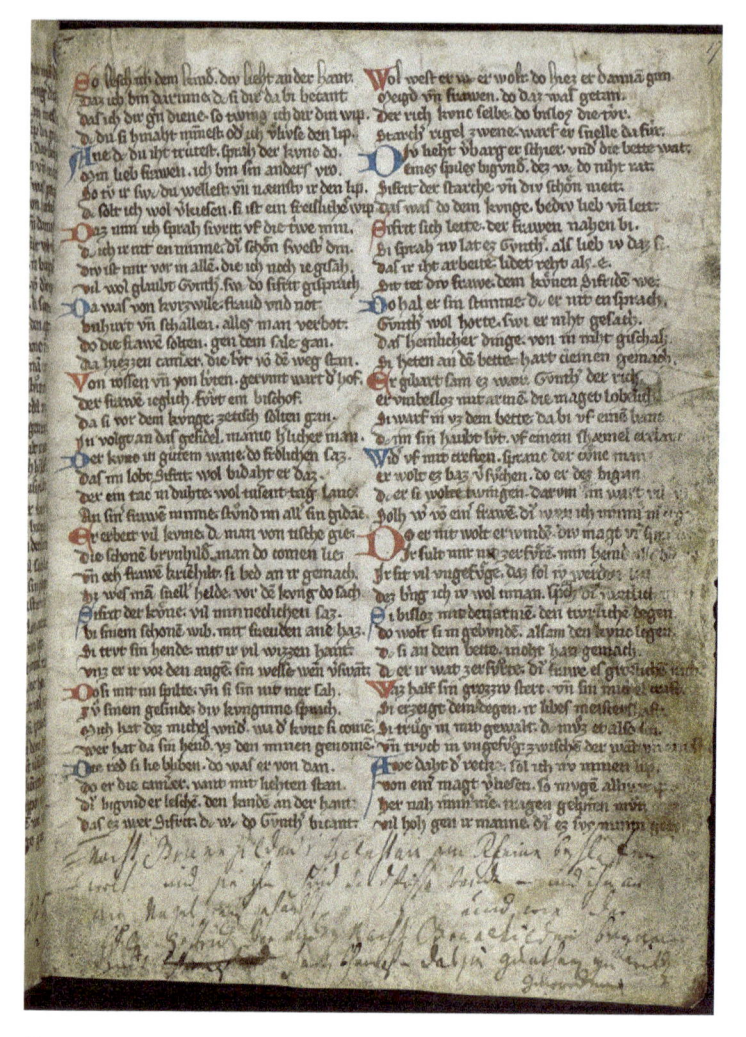

Illustration 5: Berlin, Staatsbibliothek, Germ. Fol. 474 (ms. I), fol. 17r.

The strophes correspond to 651-670 of the Codex Sangallensis 857 (ms. B) and belong to the tenth *aventiüre* of Brünhild's reception in Worms. The addition at the bottom of the page was penned by Count Karl Mohr who introduced into the Obermontani manuscript, which at the time belonged to him, several annotations, dating them Latsch, 22 July 1797. The annotation appearing on 17r, which continues from 16v, reads as follows: '[*Wie Khonig Günther von Burgund die feste=*]*=nacht Brunehilden von Iselnstain am Rheine beschlafen wolt und sie ihm Händ und Füsse bande – und ihn an ain*

Nagel aufgehankht und wie der edele Siffrid der anderen Nacht Brunehilden bezwang mit hartem Khampfe das sie Günthern zu willen geworden' ('How King Gunther of Burgundy upon his wedding night on the Rhine desired to sleep with Brünhild of Isenstein and how she tied up his hands and feet and hung him up on a nail and how the gallant Siegfried the following night compelled Brünhild in a violent struggle to give in to Gunther's will'). A full transcription of Mohr's annotations may be found in Jürgen Rabe, *Die Sprache der Berliner Nibelungenlied-Handschrift J (Ms. germ. Fol. 474)*, Göppingen, Alfred Kümmerle, 1972, pp. 250-252.

Illustration 6: The palas of Obermontani Castle. Photograph: John Butcher

*Illustration 7: Books in the exhibition from the Taylorian collection.
Photograph: Philip Flacke*

Philip Flacke
The *Nibelungenlied* as 'German *Iliad*'

If you had been a child at a German secondary school in the latter half of the nineteenth century, you might well have been asked to write an essay on the following question (as suggested for this purpose in an 1879 collection of possible topics): 'Can the *Nibelungenlied* and *Gudrun* rightly be called the German *Iliad* and *Odyssey*?'[1] Or, if you had been an American child in the US, you might have had to read about Siegfried and Kriemhilda in a school book entitled *The Story of the German Iliad* from 1892.[2] By this time, the idea of likening the *Nibelungenlied* to Homer's *Iliad* (and sometimes the *Kudrun*, the other great thirteenth-century German epic, to Homer's *Odyssey*) had been a well-established trope for over a century. How did it come about? What role does it play that it can be found in a school setting? And what does it actually signify to call the *Nibelungenlied* a 'German *Iliad*'?

Both the modern reception of the *Nibelungenlied* and the German Grecophilia that would go on to influence Goethe and the bourgeoisie of the nineteenth century, can be argued to have a common starting point: the year 1755.[3] In Dresden, Johann Joachim Winckelmann published his *Thoughts on the Imitation of Greek Works in Painting and the Art of Sculpture* inviting his German readers to identify with the people of Homer and to follow their example. At the same time, the German physician Jacob Hermann Obereit uncovered what was to be known as the Donaueschingen manuscript C of

---

[1] 'Verdienen Nibelungenlied und Gudrun mit Recht die deutsche Ilias und Odyssee genannt zu werden?' Hermann Kluge, *Themata zu deutschen Aufsätzen und Vorträgen, für höhere Unterrichtsanstalten* (Altenburg ²1879), p. 29.

[2] Mary E. Burt, *The Story of the German Iliad, A School Reader for the Sixth and Seventh Grades* (New York 1892).

[3] E.g. Joachim Heinzle, *Die Nibelungen, Lied und Sage* (Darmstadt 2005), pp. 109–10. A comprehensive bibliography of the reception of the *Nibelungenlied* with a wealth of other resources on https://www.nibelungenrezeption.de/

the *Nibelungenlied* in a palace library in Vorarlberg after the text had almost been forgotten in the sixteenth and seventeenth centuries. Obereit informed the Swiss critic Johann Jakob Bodmer about his find, who then went on to publish part of the text both in Middle High German and in translation. Bodmer had already influenced a new perception of Homer in the German speaking world.[4] On encounter with the *Nibelungenlied*, he recognised something in it that reminded him of the Homeric epics, especially the *Iliad*. Bodmer's publications on the subject can be seen as an ongoing project of 'Homerising' the *Nibelungenlied*, of assimilating it to his ideas of the Ancient Greek epics. His impulse of looking at the medieval epic through the eyes of Homer provided a starting point for a shared reception of these texts and the stories they tell.

For Bodmer and his contemporaries, connecting to the epic texts – and making connections between them – was in many ways a question of metrics. The quest for the German hexameter occupied writers from different generations, some of whom contributed passages from both *Iliad* and *Odyssey* in periodicals for public assessment.[5] Not only was the *Nibelungenlied* adapted in the metre of Homer on three different occasions Homer was translated into German in ways that imitated the form of the *Nibelungenlied*.[6]

---

[4] Annegret Pfalzgraf, *Eine Deutsche Ilias? Homer und das 'Nibelungenlied' bei Johann Jakob Bodmer. Zu den Anfängen der nationalen Nibelungenrezeption im 18. Jahrhundert* (Marburg 2003), pp. 7–60; Günter Häntzschel, 'Der deutsche Homer vom 16. bis zum 19. Jahrhundert' in *Übersetzung, Translation, Traduction, Ein internationales Handbuch zur Übersetzungsforschung*, vol. 3 (Berlin and Boston 2011), pp. 2423–27, here p. 2424; Sotera Fornaro, 'Homer in der deutschen Literatur' in *Homer-Handbuch. Leben, Werk, Wirkung* (Stuttgart and Weimar 2011), pp. 358–70, here p. 359.

[5] Günter Häntzschel, 'Die Ausbildung der deutschen Literatursprache des 18. Jahrhunderts durch Übersetzungen. Homer-Verdeutschungen als produktive Kraft' in *Mehrsprachigkeit in der deutschen Aufklärung* (Hamburg 1985), pp. 117–32.

[6] By Ferdinand Wilhelm Karl Rinne in 1860 (*Ilias*), by Ernst Johann Jakob Engel in 1885 (*Odyssey*), and by Julius Schultz in 1901 (*Ilias*). Cf. Hans-Joachim Jakob, 'Deutsche Homer-Übersetzungen seit der frühen Neuzeit. Bibliographische Übersicht' in *Homer und die deutsche Literatur* (München 2010), pp. 290–98.

Making the *Nibelungenlied* a 'German *Iliad*' was always a political enterprise. Annegret Pfalzgraf has shown that already in the Seven Years' War, shortly after its resurfacing in Vorarlberg, a patriotic agenda played a role in how the story of Siegfried and Kriemhild was talked about.[7] Carlyle later claimed the *Nibelungenlied* for 'us English *teutones*'.[8] Its nationalist and antisemitic reception culminated in the years when 'Dolchstoß' and 'Nibelungentreue' entered the language of the Third Reich, but does not end in 1945.

Violence and war are prevailing topics of all three epics – as is sex. Nevertheless, and sometimes no doubt partly because of their militaristic appeal, the stories have often been told to children. Again, it is worthwhile to ask why and how this was done and to look at parallels in the reception. Such popular retellings often do not limit themselves to the *Nibelungenlied*, but merge different texts and subjects including Old Norse literature or even Wagner, thus constructing a homogenous 'Germanic' mythology that is ultimately a product of the eighteenth and nineteenth centuries.

Aiming at younger readers or wider audiences, a number of writers published accounts of the lives of both Siegfried *and* the Homeric heroes. Gustav Schwab, famous for his *Gods and Heroes: Myths and Epics of Ancient Greece* (*Die schönsten Sagen des klassischen Alterthums*, 1838–40), had first written a different book that started with the story of the Horned Siegfried ('Der gehörnte Siegfried' in *Buch der schönsten Geschichten und Sagen*, also under the title *Die deutschen Volksbücher*, 1836–37). Helene Otto published versions of the *Odyssey*, the *Iliad*, and *Die Nibelungen* in the language of ten-year-olds (1903/04). The German author Franz Fühmann adapted both the *Nibelungenlied* (in 1971 and 1973) and the Homeric epics (numerous times). Anglophone authors like Padraic Colum (*The Adventure of Odysseus* 1918, *The Children of Odin* 1920) and Barbara Leonie Picard (*The Odyssey of Homer* 1952, *German Hero-Sagas and Folk-Tales* 1958, *The Iliad of Homer* 1960) likewise published children's books

---

[7] Cf. Pfalzgraf, *Eine Deutsche Ilias?*, pp. 118–136.
[8] In 1831. Cf. Mary Boyle's essay in this book.

on both Greek and 'Germanic' mythology. Sometimes, such accounts appeared as part of the same series, as in the case of the books entitled *Told to the Children*, which are part of the exhibition.

While academic translations were historically monopolised by men, a substantial part of children's books on Homer and the Nibelungen were contributed by women. Today, we witness a trend in literary retellings of myth, often written from feminist perspectives. Being intensely discussed on BookTok and other social media, these accounts do not limit themselves to children's literature. Especially in the anglophone world, various writers are following earlier examples of novels by Mary Renault, Margaret Atwood, Madeline Miller, and others, focusing on women and marginalised voices, and rereading Homer from queer and postcolonial perspectives.[9] The *Nibelungenlied*, too, has in the last years prompted contemporary reimaginings by writers like Ulrike Draesner and Felicitas Hoppe. The reception of Homer and the Nibelungen is very much a matter of today.

The exhibition reveals the different stages and trends, the key impulses, and some idiosyncratic approaches to the translation and adaption of the *Iliad*, the *Odyssey*, and the *Nibelungenlied*. It showcases material from the Taylor Institution Library's collections, alongside additions from the Bodleian Library and some items on private loan. Building on the 2022 exhibition 'Violent Victorian Medievalism', curated by Mary Boyle, it shines particular light on adaptations for children and to the fraught topic of women and violence. The books featured tell the story of the various attempts to assert ownership of these epics. This was not simply a matter of translating the texts, but of claiming them for different national and pre-national identities, for specific ideas of masculinity and femininity, and for militaristic agendas and racist ideologies. But also, more recently, the epics have been retold with feminist, queer, and anti-colonial causes in mind. Maybe that can be the subject for another exhibition.

---

[9] For postcolonial perspectives cf. Emily Greenwood, 'Postcolonial Perceptions of Homeric Epic' in *The Cambridge Guide to Homer* (Cambridge 2020), pp. 532–35.

Appendix: 'A German *Iliad*' Endorsements and Critique

Es ist eine Art von Ilias, und wenigstens etwas, so die Grundlage einer Ilias in sich enthält.

> Bodmer in a letter to his friend Laurenz Zellweger (24 August 1755), shortly after getting to know the *Nibelungenlied*.

Dieses Gedicht hat etwas iliadisches, dem an der Vollkommenheit, die in der Epopöe erfordert wird, nicht viel abgehet.

> Bodmer (?) 1757 in an announcement of the upcoming partial edition of the *Nibelungenlied* (*Freymüthige Nachrichten*, pp. 74–75).

Alle diese Stücke habe ich abgeschnitten, und ich glaube mit demselben Rechte, mit welchem Homer die Entführung der Helena, die Aufopferung der Iphigenia, und alle Begegnisse der zehn Jahre, die vor dem Zwiste zwischen Achilles und Agamemnon vorhergegangen sind, weggelassen hat, auf die er nur bey Gelegenheiten sich als auf bekannte Sachen beziehet.

> Bodmer in the preface to his partial *Nibelungenlied* edition *Chriemhilden Rache, Und Die Klage. Zwey Heldengedichte Aus dem schvväbischen Zeitpuncte* (1757), p. VII.

Die Dapferkeit erscheint hier in einer wunderbaren Verschiedenheit bey verschiedenen Personen; eine andere ist Rüdegers, eine andere Blödelins, eine andere Hagenen, des Volkers, Dieterichs von Bern – In der Beschreibung der Kämpfe herrschet eine Mannigfaltigkeit von Begegnissen, so daß schwerlich ein Kampf, ein Gefecht, dem andern gleich ist. Jedes neue Gefecht erhebt sich über das vorhergehende an Grösse, Gefahr, und Verwirrung. – Das sind Eigenschaften, die sonst dem Homer zugehören. Der Poet hat auch dieses mit dem Griechen mehr als so mancher anderer Poet gemein, daß er uns selten an den Poeten gedenken läßt; er nimmt uns allein mit seiner Handlung ein, und machet uns aus Lesern zu Hörern.

> Bodmer in the preface to his partial *Nibelungenlied* edition (1757), pp. VII–VIII.

Die Klage ist ein besonderes Gedicht und ebenfalls von der epischen oder erzählenden Art, wiewol die Handlung darinnen größtentheils Leiden ist.

Es hat einige Ähnlichkeit mit dem lezten Gesang der Ilias, wo die Klagen der Andromache, der Hecuba, und der Helena, und Hectors Leichenbegängniß vorkommen.

> Bodmer in the preface to his partial *Nibelungenlied* edition (1757), p. VIII.

Ueberhaupt giebt der Poet seinen vornehmsten Personen Empfindungen von Ehre, Großmuth, und Redlichkeit, die wir bey Homers Helden nicht in demselben offenbaren Lichte antreffen.

> Bodmer in the preface to his partial *Nibelungenlied* edition (1757), p. VIII.

Man siehet keinen Anschein, daß er jemals werde ganz gedrukt werden. Es ist in der That für den Ruhm des schwäbischen Zeitpunktes am besten gesorget, wenn man nicht alles, was noch in dem Staube verborgen liget, an den Tag hervorziehet, sondern in dem, was man uns giebt, eine reife und einsichtsvolle Wahl beobachtet. Das Ausnehmende in dieser alten Literatur ist eben nicht im Ueberflusse übrig.

> Bodmer in the preface to his partial *Nibelungenlied* edition (1757), p. X, about the two thirds of the text which he had cut.

Bodmers Verherrlichung des Stoffes und der Vergleich mit dem Maß aller Dinge, der Homerischen Ilias, sind als Ursprung der nationalen Auslegung des Nibelungenmythos zu sehen.

> Tobias Hermann Kehm in his book *Der Nibelungenmythos im Ersten Weltkrieg. Die Entstehung kontrafaktischer Narrationen und deren Wirkung auf das Geschichtsbewusstsein* (2015), p. 29.

Eh die aonischen Musen in Deutschlands hainen gewandelt,
Als Achilles noch nicht in deutschen gesängen gefochten,
Und Ulysses die freyer noch nicht im bettler betrogen,
Sangen die Eschilbache, von deutschen Musen begeistert,
Eigne gesänge, die frucht des selbst erfindenden geistes.
Einer von ihnen sang mit Mäonides tone die schwester,
Welcher die brüder den theueen [sic] gemahl erschlugen, die schwester
Wieder die brüder erschlug. Die zeit hat den nahmen getilget,

Aber sein lied gerettet, ich hab' es gehört, und ich will es
Lauter singen, es soll vom Rhein zur Ostsee ertönen.

> Bodmer's proem, which, in Homeric manner, he added to his partial translation of the *Nibelungenlied* entitled *Die Rache der Schwester* (1767).

Der Nibelungen Lied könnte die teutsche Ilias werden.

> The Swiss historian Johannes Müller in the second volume of his Swiss history, *Der Geschichten schweizerischer Eidgenossenschaft Anderes Buch* (1786), p. 121.

Der Akzent liegt auf dem Konjunktiv, denn Müller verlangte analog zur homerischen eine eigene Nibelungenphilologie [...].

> Otfrid Ehrismann (2002), p. 171, on the former quotation in a standard textbook about the epoch and the reception of the *Nibelungenlied*.

Voß soll sich sehr hart gegen dich bei der Rudolphi über dich ausgelassen haben, weil diese ihm erzahlte, auch du habest von den Nibelungen gesagt, sie konnten uns gewissermassen, waß den Griechen der Homer sein, er sagte unter andern, daß heiße einen Saustall einem Pallast vergleichen [...]

> Clemens Brentano in a letter to Achim von Arnim, written between 1 and 5 October 1805.

Von J. H. Voss wird berichtet, daß er das Nibelungenlied in seiner Schule zu Eurin im Auszuge lesen ließ.

> Hermann Leopold Köster in his *Geschichte der deutschen Jugendliteratur* (^{3}1920), p. 233.

Schöpfer unsterblicher Namen, obgleich selbst namelos, Grab sey
    Erd' oder Ozean dir,
Erd' und Ozean halten dich nicht, dein gewaltiger Geist fuhr
    Auf zu der Halle des Lichts,
Deren goldene Pforte des tuscischen Dantes gedreyter
    Schlüssel eröffnet und schliesst;
Wo am Throne Homerus, Parthenias, Virgil, den Finger
    Uber die Lippe gelegt,
Majestätisch in Demut den spätern Machtton der Miltons
    Harfe entrauschet, behorcht:

> Dir an der Seite sizt dort, der uns dich erklärte, der Sänger
> Noahs, noch selbst unerklärt;
> Ja Ihm danken wir es, dass in Sivrit ein bessrer Achilleus
> Wieder vom Grabe erstand.
> Zwar keiner Göttin Sohn, doch würdiger Halbgott zu heissen
> Als den dein Meister uns sang!
> War nicht Homerus dein Meister? Die Funken homerischer Geister
> Wehn in des Nibelungs Nacht.
> Lächelt ewig auf Andromaches Wange die Thräne?
> Weinet nicht Chremhild wie sie?
>> Johann Heinrich Füssli's poem 'Der Dichter der Schwesterrache' on the anonymous poet of the *Nibelungenlied* (1800/1810), qtd. in Joachim Heinzle's anthology *Mythos Nibelungen* (2013), p. 201. 'The singer of Noah' ('der Sänger Noahs') refers to Bodmer, who had written an epic about the patriarch (*Noah, ein Heldengedicht* 1750/52).

> In dem geflügelten Wohllaut der Sprache und des Versbaues, in den sich so lieblich an alle Dinge und ihre Eigenschaften anschmiegenden Benennungen, auch in der Ruhe und Besonnenheit, der Reinheit der epischen Form, ist Homer unerreichbar. Was aber Lebendigkeit und Gegenwart der Darstellung, dann die Größe der Leidenschaften, Charaktere, und der ganzen Handlung betrifft, darf sich das Lied der Nibelungen kühnlich mit der Ilias messen, ich würde sagen, es thut es ihr zuvor, wenn man es sich nicht zum Gesetze machen müßte, nie ein Meisterwerk auf Unkosten des andern zu loben.
>> August Wilhelm Schlegel in his Berlin lectures on the *History of Romantic Literature* (*Geschichte der romantischen Litteratur*) 1802/03.

> Fast hätte ich das beste Vergessen, Tieck hat mir seine trefliche Bearbeitung, und Ergänzung des Niebelungen Liedes, des einzigen uns wirklich angehörenden Epos vorgelesen, es erregt einen Eindruck uns selbst herrlicher und größer als Homer, und die ganze Zeit (dunkle) um Atila ist hell und klar, es hat bewiesen, daß es historisch Wahr ist, es ist sein größtes Verdienst, diese Wiederherstellung.
>> Clemens Brentano in a letter to Friedrich Karl von Savigny, early March 1805.

Der wesentliche Vortheil also, den die Annahme unsers Vorschlages gewähren würde, das Lied der Nibelungen zu einem Hauptbuche der

Erziehung zu machen, es gründlich in den Schulen zu erklären und dem Gedächtnisse der Jugend einzuprägen, wäre der, den Geschichten unsers Volkes einen dichterischen Hintergrund zu geben, woran es ihnen bisher ganz und gar gefehlt hat. Von dieser Seite kann dieß Werk für uns eben das werden, was Homer den Griechen war.

> A. W. Schlegel 1812 in *Deutsches Museum*, p. 32.

Wie der einzelne Mensch so auch die Nation ruht auf dem Altvorhandenen, Ausländischen oft mehr als auf dem Eigenen, Ererbten und Selbstgeleisteten; aber nur in so fern ein Volk eigene Literatur hat, kann es urtheilen und versteht die vergangene wie die gleichzeitige Welt. [...] Der Deutsche war auf gutem Weg und wird ihn gleich wieder finden, sobald er das schädliche Bestreben aufgibt, die Nibelungen der Ilias gleichzustellen.

> Goethe 1817 in his periodical *Über Kunst und Altertum*, qtd. in Gunter E. Grimm, 'Goethe und das Nibelungenlied, Eine Dokumentation' (2006).

Haben wir Deutsche nicht unsern herrlichen Nibelungen durch solche Vergleichung den größten Schaden gethan?

> Goethe 1819 in his 'Noten und Abhandlungen' to his *West–östlicher Divan*, qtd. in Grimm (2006).

Und wie euch erst Homer gesungen
Erfreut ihr euch der Nibelungen

> Goethe in a fragment dating 1821, qtd. in Grimm (2006).

Das Klassische nenne ich das Gesunde, und das Romantische das Kranke. Und da sind die Nibelungen klassisch wie der Homer, denn beide sind gesund und tüchtig.

> Goethe 1821, in conversation with Johann Peter Eckermann, qtd. in Grimm (2006).

Ilias und *Odyssee* bleiben unterschöpflich ... An Folgen aus den *Nibelungen* fehlt es uns nicht, und ich denke daran, daß sie zu überbieten sind; denn meist werden die Heldengestalten des Mittelalters nur als travestierte Wesen des höhern griechischen Stils anzusehen sein.

> Goethe 1830, qtd. in Hartmut Fröschle, *Goethes Verhältnis zur Romantik* (2002), p. 477.

Die Jugend, aus sich selbst, nimmt keinen Antheil daran, wie an Homer. Und wer mir das widerspricht, der wird seine Erfahrung unter dem Bedenken zurücknehmen müssen, daß, wo ja die Nibelungen erklärt werden, es meist durch einen begeisterten Kenner geschieht, dessen Antheil und vielleicht geistvolle, gewiß aber liebevolle Behandlung mehr fesselt als die Sache selbst, während Homer das einzige Buch der Welt ist, dem in einem irgend sinnigen Knaben auch die Mishandlung des ärgsten Pedanten nur wenigen Schaden thut. Wenn man uns doch nicht mit dem schönen Gedanken einer Nationalerziehung ködern und fangen wollte! Eine Nation, die die Bibel und den Homer zu ihren Erziehungsbüchern gemacht hat, die sich am besten Mark der ganzen Menschheit nähren will, eine solche Nation kann einem solchen Werke, wie die Nibelungen, keinen so bevorzugenden Rang unter ihren Bildungs- und Unterrichtsmitteln gönnen; sie bleibt trotz ewigen Widersprüchen der Klüglinge auf dem betretenen Wege mit fester Ausdauer, während die Begeisterung für unsre alten Poesien von heute und gestern ist, und aus Zeiten die von einer Deutschthümelei befallen waren, über die wir mit kaltem Blute lachen.

In his *History of the Germans' National Literature* (*Geschichte der poetischen National-Literatur der Deutschen* 1835, here p. 272), Georg Gottfried Gervinus includes a digression, in which he argues against the idea of the 'German *Iliad*' and against the notion of reading the *Nibelungenlied* in lower grades in school.

Dem Knaben, dem werdenden Menschen, können die Helden der Nibelungen die achäischen des Homer nicht ersetzen. Die Strebsamkeit, das Feuer, das Vertrauen auf menschliche Kraft, von dem diese beseelt sind, kann allein Menschen von tüchtiger Art bilden, die Passivität dieser alten Germanen, die ihre heidnische Unruhe schon mit einer gewissen Schläfrigkeit vertauscht haben, kann uns nicht das Geschlecht schaffen, das den gegenwärtigen Zeiten gegenüber nothwendig ist.

Gervinus 1835, p. 273.

Wir fühlen uns schwerlich diesen Burgundern verwandter, als den Achäern des Homer, die uns doch noch Liebe zum Vaterlande lehren können, für das im ganzen Mittelalter nicht einmal der Name existirt. Wenn man vollends den poetischen Werth im vaterländischen Dünkel dem Homer entgegenzustellen kühn genug war, so muß man bedauern, daß so wenig

Kunstsinn unter uns herrscht, daß Aussprüche der Art nur eine Möglichkeit sind [...]
> Gervinus 1835, p. 273.

Mit Recht sind Nibelungen und Kudrun in einem ähnlichen Verhältniss aufgefasst worden wie Ilias und Odyssee. Der großartige Hintergrund macht jene wie die Nibelungen gewaltiger und erschütternder; die Schicksale von ganzen Völkern werden mit dem Schwerte entschieden, ein Herrscherhaus, dem edle Helden angehören, geht vor unsern Augen dem Untergange entgegen. Aber auch die Sieger erfreuen sich des Glückes nicht; das Schicksal ist auch über sie hereingebrochen. Das Ganze athmet den Geist einer Tragödie, und mehr noch als in dem griechischen tritt in dem deutschen Epos dieser zum Tragischen sich gipfelnde Charakter hervor. Alles gewinnt dramatisches Leben: mit fieberhafter Spannung wird der Hörer durch alle Stufen des sicherschreitenden Verderbens geführt. 'Nach Freude Leid', ist der ernste Klang, der durch das ganze Nibelungenlied hindurchgeht [...]
> Karl Bartsch in his edition of the *Kudrun* (1865), pp. xv–xvi.

Verdienen Nibelungenlied und Gudrun mit Recht die deutsche Ilias und Odyssee genannt zu werden?
> Hermann Kluge, *Themata zu deutschen Aufsätzen und Vorträgen, für höhere Unterrichtsanstalten* (^{2}1879), p. 29.

The [book] is an attempt to popularize for children the substance of the old Nibelungen Lied, the national poem of the Germans. An immense amount of ingenuity, learning, and research has been spent in determining the origin of this lay, which stands to the German race much as Homer stands to the Greeks and the legend of Arthur to us.
> Review of Lydia Hands' *Golden Threads from an Ancient Loom*, 'Christmas Books', *The Times*, 16/12/1879.

Modern German critics agree in assigning a high literary value to the poem of Gu-drun [sic], and compare it not unfavorably with the Nibelungen Lied. Bartsch, the critic above named, says: "The general impression which the poem gives is one of greater beauty, though not always of equal grandeur with that of the Nibelungen; it is a worthy companion-piece. The two are justly compared, as are the Iliad and the Odyssey. In the Nibelungen as in the Iliad the fate of a whole people is decided by the sword, and the ruling house, consisting of noble heroes, meets destruction before our eyes; but the conquerors do not fully rejoice in their success. The whole breathes a tragic spirit, even more than the Greek epic. 'Nach Freude Leid' – 'after joy comes sorrow' – is the earnest tone throughout. [...]"

> This extract from Bartsch's introduction to his edition of *Kudrun* appeared in the first full English translation of that text: Mary Pickering Nichols, *Gudrun: A Medieval Epic* (1889), p. v.

It is truly wonderful, with what skill our simple untaught Poet deals with the marvellous; admitting it without reluctance or criticism, yet precisely in the degree and shape that will best avail him. Here, if in no other respect, we should say that he has a decided superiority to Homer himself. ... The Singer of the 'Nibelungen' is a far different person from Homer; far inferior both in culture and in genius. Nothing of the glowing imagery, of the fierce, bursting energy, of the mingled fire and gloom, that dwell in the old Greek, makes its appearance here. The German Singer is comparatively a simple nature; has never penetrated deep into life; never 'questioned Fate'; or struggled with fearful mysteries; of all which we find traces in Homer, still more in Shakespeare; but with meek, believing submission, has taken the Universe as he found it represented to him; and rejoices with a fine childlike gladness in the mere outward shows of things.

> Thomas Carlyle, *Westminster Review*, 1831

In conclusion, we must again say how strange it seems to us, that this Volsung Tale, which is in fact an unversified poem, should never before have been translated into English. For this is the Great Story of the North, which should be to all our race what the Tale of Troy was to the Greeks – to all our race first, and afterwards, when the change of the world has made our race nothing more than a name of what has been – a story too – then should it be to those that come after us no less than the Tale of Troy has been to us.

> William Morris and Eiríkr Magnússon in the preface to their book *Völsunga Saga: The Story of the Volsungs and Niblungs, with Certain Songs from the Elder Edda* (1870), p. xi.

My dear Boys and Girls,

> You are sure to like Sigurd, or Siegfried, by whichever name you choose to call him. He is the model of manliness. His wife, Gudrun,

or Kriemhild, you will pity and, for her sorrows, in pitying her you will forgive her for her cruel revenge.

As to the whole story, you cannot help liking that if you are a true child of the North for, as William Morris has said, it is 'the Great Story of the North which should be to all our race what the Tale of Troy was to the Greeks,' and, as Thomas Carlyle said, 'it has meaning and charms for us.'

> From Thomas Cartwright's short preface to his children's book *Sigurd the Dragon Slayer: A Twice-Told Tale* (1907).

In the place they occupy in the national literature and in the relation which they bear to one another, the German *Nibelungenlied* and the *Gudrun* resemble the *Iliad* and the *Odyssey* of the Greeks. In the *Nibelungenlied* the tragic fate of Troy has its counterpart in the total extinction of the Burgundians, while in both the *Odyssey* and the *Gudrun* the accompaniment to battles and adventures is always the beat of the waves

> Margaret Armour, *Gudrun* (1928), p. v.

[...] es war sein Unglück, daß es erst zusammen mit der Wiederentdeckung Homers, Mitte des 18. Jahrhunderts, ins Bewußtsein der deutschen Kultur zurückkehrte. Dadurch wurde es von Anfang an als 'deutsche Ilias' festgelegt, und dieser zunächst plausibel erscheinende Vergleich war für das NL bald mörderisch, denn es handelt sich, obwohl beides Dichtungen von Weltrang sind, um zwei grundverschiedene Dinge [...]

> Franz Fühmann in the concept for a film adaptation of the *Nibelungenlied*, which he submitted in 1971 to the GDR film studio DEFA, qtd. in *Der Nibelunge Not* (1993), p. 151.

*Illustration 8: Poster for 'Violent Victorian Medievalism'.
Design by Katherine Beard, Linacre College, Oxford*

Mary Boyle
The Victorian *Nibelungenlied*

The essay brings two themes together of the reception of the *Nibelungenlied* which, *mutatis mutandis*, also apply to the adaptation of the Homeric poems in the Victorian era: the fascination with medieval violence and the difficulty in translating this for children.[1]

Violent Victorian Medievalism

> medievalism, *n.*
> 'the reception, interpretation or recreation of the European Middle Ages in post-medieval cultures', Louise D'Arcens, 2016[2]

A portcullis creaks. Dismembered corpses litter the snow. An unwashed man dismounts and looks on in terror. Just minutes into the first episode of *Game of Thrones* (HBO, 2011–19), the scene is set. This world, visually coded as medieval, is brutal. Such a trope crops up again and again in contemporary popular culture, often clearly taking a lead from HBO's era-defining series. Even puppets were beheaded in the teaser for *The Green Knight* (A24, 2021), while trailers for other medievalist films and television programmes over the past decade repeatedly emphasise barbarity and bloodshed: *Vikings* (History, 2013–), *The Last Kingdom* (BBC, Netflix, 2015–), *Outlaw King* (Netflix, 2018). One of the latest iterations is called, simply, *Medieval* (WOG FILM s.r.o., 2022). But despite defending the violence

---

[1] The first essay was published as 'Violent Medievalism, Violent Victorians' as part of the volume 'Violent Victorian Medievalism', ed. by Mary Boyle, Oxford 2022, the second as 'Translating Medieval Violence: What's Acceptable for Children?' by Mary Boyle on the Queen's Translation Exchange blog in 2021, and then in the catalogue of the 'Violent Victorian Medievalism' exhibition. Reissued with permission.

[2] Louise D'Arcens, 'Introduction: Medievalism: scope and complexity', in *The Cambridge Companion to Medievalism* (Cambridge, 2016), pp. 1–13.

in *A Song of Ice and Fire / Game of Thrones* by saying, 'It's not the Disneyland Middle Ages', George R.R. Martin did not rip the Band-Aid off a shared vision of a utopian Middle Ages to reveal historically accurate and hitherto unexplored gore. In truth, the idea that 'medieval' is a synonym for violent, even when not explicitly articulated, runs through later responses to the period, from the cerebral to the popular.

Enter the Victorians. A fascination with the Middle Ages shaped public life in the nineteenth century – and in exchange, it reshaped the Middle Ages into a form still dominant today. Englishness became inextricably connected with a reimagined medieval past expressed through art, architecture, and literature. English traits and values were traced to a Golden Age of chivalry, and a national character was anchored in a heroic so-called Germanic past (also described as Anglo-Saxon, Northern, or Teutonic). The longevity of this tradition is evident in the 2021 St George's Day Google Doodle.[3] But chivalry and heroism necessarily exist within a martial context, and violence already permeated the geopolitics, literature, and culture of Britain's 'imperial century'. Abroad, Britain added 400 million people and 10 million square miles to its Empire, at the cost of countless lives.[4] At home, cheap and garishly illustrated penny dreadfuls sold in huge numbers thanks to rising literacy rates and an increased appetite for entertainment.[5] This taste for melodrama gave rise to the sensation novel which – supposedly – had a more respectable audience. It catered, though, to an equivalent taste for bloodshed.[6] Medieval or medieval-adjacent literature offered another respectable vehicle for violence. In the 1830s, Thomas Carlyle published an essay

---

[3] '23 April 2021: St. George's Day 2021', *Google*, 2021.
[4] Timothy Parsons, *The British Imperial Century, 1815-1914: A World History Perspective* (Lanham, Boulder, New York, Toronto, and Oxford, 1999), p. 3.
[5] For more information on the penny dreadful, see Judith Flanders, 'Victorian Penny Dreadfuls', brewminate, 2019.
[6] For more information on sensation novels, see Matthew Sweet, *Inventing the Victorians* (2001).

drawing the nation's attention to a medieval epic, 'belong[ing] especially to us English *Teutones*'.[7] This was the *Nibelungenlied*, a story of love, betrayal, vengeance, and hopeless heroism. It had already been decreed a potential 'German *Iliad*' – and, like the *Iliad*, its body count was vast.[8] With its frequent scenes of graphic violence and potential for ethnonationalist identity construction, the narrative incorporated various national pursuits for the Victorians. They revelled in it, as did the Edwardians – right up to the First World War.

The *Nibelungenlied*

> Uns ist in alten mæren wunders vil geseit
> von helden lobebæren, von grôzer arebeit,
> von frouden, hôchgeziten, von weinen und von klagen,
> von küener recken strîten muget ir nu wunder hœren sagen
> *The Nibelungenlied*, stanza 1
>
> In ancient tales, we are told much of wonder: of praiseworthy heroes, of great toil, of joys, festivals, of tears and laments, and of brave warriors battling, now you may hear wonders told.

The *Nibelungenlied* is the most famous German version of a collection of heroic legends known also in various Scandinavian incarnations. It tells of the dragon-slaying hero Siegfried and his arrival in Burgundy, where he hopes to woo the famously beautiful Princess Kriemhild. Various obstacles – or opportunities to prove himself – present themselves. He fights off invading Danes and Saxons and, through dishonest means, helps Kriemhild's brother Gunther win the hand of the warrior queen, Brünhild, after which Siegfried and Kriemhild are also married. Years later, while Siegfried and Kriemhild are visiting Burgundy, tensions erupt, and Gunther conspires with his vassal, Hagen, to have Siegfried murdered. Hagen stabs him in the back while they are hunting in the forest, and leaves his body

---

[7] Thomas Carlyle, 'Das Nibelungen Lied, übersetzt von Karl Simrock (The "Nibelungen Lied", translated by Karl Simrock.) 2 Vols. 12mo. Berlin. 1827.', *Westminster Review*, 15/29 (1831), p. 4. See the essay by Philip Flacke in this volume.

[8] Johannes von Müller, *Der Geschichten schweizerischer Eidgenoschaft. Anderes Buch. Von dem Aufblühen der ewigen Bünde* (Leipzig, 1786), II, p. 121.

outside Kriemhild's door. Hagen then steals her treasure hoard, a gift from Siegfried, and sinks it in the Rhine, ostensibly to prevent her from using it to gain allies in pursuit of revenge.

Years pass, and Kriemhild accepts a marriage proposal from Etzel, King of the Huns, hoping to find an opportunity to avenge Siegfried. She invites the Burgundians to visit her and engineers an outbreak of violence. Ultimately, almost nobody is left alive, and Gunther and Hagen, the last surviving Burgundians, are brought before her. She orders her brother to be killed and brings his head to Hagen, before decapitating Hagen with Siegfried's sword. A bystander, outraged that this fearsome warrior has been killed by a woman, strikes Kriemhild down himself, and the poet concludes:

> Ine kan iu niht bescheiden, waz sider dâ geschach,
> wan ritter und vrouwen weinen man dá sach,
> dar zuo die edeln knehte, ir lieben friunde tôt.
> dâ hât daz mære ein ende. diz ist der Nibelunge nôt.
> *The Nibelungenlied*, stanza 2376
>
> I cannot tell you what happened there later, only that knights and ladies were seen weeping, noble squires too, their dear friends dead. Here the story has an end: this is the Nibelungs' distress.

After Carlyle's essay, anglophone adaptations began to appear, initially as a trickle and then, following the first performances of Richard Wagner's *Ring des Nibelungen*, as a flood. Writers often adapted not only the *Nibelungenlied* itself, but combined it with the other Scandinavian and German narratives associated with its characters, and introduced elements from their own imaginations – just as Wagner had done. The resulting adaptations were aimed at all age groups and educational levels, and many were eye-catchingly illustrated. While the slightest allusion to sex was usually avoided in Victorian and Edwardian adaptations (as opposed to translations) of this material, gruesome violence tended to make it through, including in those versions aimed at children. Indeed, it often appeared in picture form: a woman brandishes the decapitated head of her brother; a man is stabbed in the back while drinking from a spring; a knight faces up

The Victorian Nibelungenlied 19

to a fearsome dragon. Some illustrators stopped short of depicting the violence itself, but were happy to depict the moments immediately before or after: the spear poised to leave a hand and enter a back; piles of corpses. This predilection for carnage has echoes of modern children's educational entertainment like *Horrible Histories* (CBBC, 2009–2020, based on Terry Deary's book series, 1993-2013), which was marketed as 'history with the nasty bits left in', but it was also par for the course in the long nineteenth century (1789–1914), and was certainly not limited to the items on display in this exhibition. Lucy H. Fleming's contribution to the 2022 catalogue on children's adaptations of Chaucer, for example, casts light on another tradition of medievalist violence in the nineteenth century.

The *Nibelungenlied*, along with its associated material, however, was so widely reinterpreted in the long nineteenth century, and so emblematic for notions of a so-called Germanic identity, that it provides a useful prism through which to demonstrate the wider implications of violent Victorian (and Edwardian) medievalism.[9] Children's literature of this period routinely matched a reticence about sex with scenes of extreme violence, often while simultaneously smuggling in an educational message. In adaptations of the *Nibelungenlied* and other related legends, that message was unequivocal, both for children and for adults: this narrative is your cultural inheritance. We can thus see the connection forged between (ethno-)nationalist nostalgia and a violence that can often be parsed as heroic or fantastical, thus neutering potential charges of sensationalism. It is a clear forerunner of twentieth- and twenty-first-century children's medievalism, as well as mapping on to more recent trends in violent medievalism and popular culture.

---

[9] Because such tendencies continue beyond the strict boundaries of the Victorian era, as far as the outbreak of the First World War, the original exhibition included items published up to twelve years after Victoria's death.

Mary Boyle

Epic Adaptations for Children

Illustration 9: 'The maiden hurled her spear'
MacGregor 1908 (section 4), facing p. 76. Playmobil figure of a Viking.
Photograph: Henrike Lähnemann

Knights and dragons are such a fixture of children's literature that they seem to find their way into the least medieval settings imaginable. Not only is there even a *Postman Pat* episode on the topic but, since I started writing this, I've discovered that there are two, 'Postman Pat and the Greendale Knights' (2007) and 'Postman Pat and the King's Armour' (2017). But have you ever stopped to think about how strange this is? Dragons are bloodthirsty monsters, while the business of knights is, well, violence. It might be characterised as violence in the service of their country, or to protect damsels in distress, but it's violence nonetheless. The purpose of those swords isn't simply to shine, but to kill – or at the very least to threaten to kill. And yet we think of these characters as not just child-friendly, but obvious material for children's stories. Why?

Fitting knights and their world into children's literature isn't a new idea, but goes back well over a hundred years, to Victorian and Edwardian children's authors who made use of medieval texts in their search for new material for young audiences. Drawing on the past is never politically neutral, and it certainly wasn't for these writers, who were getting involved in a contemporary passion for the Middle Ages which was so influential that many of the things we think of today as medieval are actually products of the nineteenth century.[10] So why wasn't this politically neutral? Countless words have been written about this, but to cut a long story short and then simplify it, there was a desire to identify the beginnings of English culture and democracy in a pre-Norman-Conquest past which was shared with other supposedly 'Germanic' (itself a complicated and loaded term) regions like Germany and Scandinavia. Given this background, maybe it's not surprising that writers at the time decided that the *Nibelungenlied* would make a perfect children's book. After all, it featured not only those knights and dragons, but also other fairy-tale staples like kings, queens, princes, princesses, treasure, prophecies, and battles.

---

[10] For more on this, see my blogpost 'The Medievalism Onion: Layers of Interpretation', *TORCH*, 2020 [accessed 11 May 2024].

Unfortunately, the *Nibelungenlied* also has pretty non-child-friendly features: sex and sexual violence; betrayal and (mass) murder; the decapitation of a child; burning people alive; drinking blood from corpses; the parading of the decapitated head of one prisoner in front of another; the beheading of an unarmed man; and – to close proceedings – the brutal killing of a woman. Basically, the knights behave like the warriors they are – but it's worth pointing out that, generally speaking, the violence itself wasn't exactly a problem for our writers. The real issue was that much of the violence is directed (and partly carried out) by a woman, our main character, Kriemhild.

Turning the *Nibelungenlied* into a children's story obviously wasn't going to be just a matter of translating it from Middle High German into English and putting it in the hands of young Victorians. The mostly fairy-tale-like first half of the narrative was quite easily adapted for children, but the second part presented many more problems because the plot basically follows Kriemhild's violent quest for revenge. Now admittedly, it could have been worse – the Scandinavian material features the female protagonist killing her children, baking them into pies, and serving them to their father. At least Kriemhild's limit was putting her son in a situation which she knew would lead to his death in order to further her revenge plot. One common solution was to adapt only the first part, perhaps summarising the revenge plot in a few sentences. These adaptations would usually bring in some Scandinavian material, which had the advantage over the German version that the fight with the dragon didn't take place 'offscreen'. This particular violence only involves a man and a monster, so it could appear in its full gory detail, including Siegfried's post-fight bath in the dragon's blood. But there were some writers who decided that they were just going to go for it and adapt the whole thing. Let's take a look at two of them.

First up, Lydia Hands, author of *Golden Threads from an Ancient Loom*, subtitled *Das Nibelungenlied, adapted to the use of young readers*. She was ahead of the curve by publishing in 1880 – most English-language children's adaptations of the *Nibelungenlied* came along after the English premiere of Wagner's *Ring* cycle in 1882 drew attention to the material. Hands deals with the difficulty of translating Kriemhild's violence by finding an explanation which would make (legal) sense to her audience: Kriemhild was mad with grief at the death of her child. You're probably thinking that this is a bit rich of Kriemhild, since this is entirely her own fault. So Hands simply neglects to translate that part of the text. In her version, the boy's death comes as a terrible shock, causing Kriemhild to faint in horror. When she wakes up, 'a frenzy, as of madness, possessed Criemhild; her enemy should not escape, even though her own life should be the penalty'. Then she orders the hall to be burned down with hundreds of men inside. It's the death of her son that triggers Kriemhild's madness, and her madness which triggers her indiscriminate violence. Insanity was a routine defence in nineteenth-century law courts, and it means that Hands can keep all the violence – and she *really* does – without undermining contemporary expectations of women. It doesn't excuse Kriemhild, and she doesn't get a happy ending, just a marginally less violent death, but it relieves her of her moral responsibility and any knock-on consequences for society.

This wasn't enough for Gertrude Schottenfels in *Stories of the Nibelungen for Young People* in 1905. There's no violent death for Kriemhild's son, and Kriemhild herself is kept at some distance from the violence. Eventually, Hagen and Gunther are brought to her by a knight, who makes her give 'her word of honor that he, and he alone, should be permitted to put them to death'. So really, when Kriemhild orders them to be beheaded 'according to the custom of these olden times', she's just following a knight's suggestion. This Kriemhild is allowed to live, and the closest we get to a condemnation is being told that she was 'once gentle and beautiful', implying that she no longer is. But she's neither dead nor disgraced, and the spectacular body count isn't attributed to her. – Maybe this is as close as we get to an answer to my starting question. Compared to the other violence in the *Nibelungenlied*, knights' (and dragons') violence isn't considered a big deal. As long as you can translate away the unacceptable violence, you can keep the rest – no matter how extreme.

Illustration 10: Franz Fühmann's film script (section 3) in the stacks of the Taylorian. Photograph: Philip Flacke

TIMOTHY POWELL
The *Nibelungenlied* from National Socialist Epic to Socialist National Epic

> Es gilt heute, das NL [*Nibelungenlied*] als Erbe überhaupt in Besitz zu nehmen. Dabei könnte ein Film eine hervorragende Rolle spielen. Es wäre ein Beitrag, den nur die sozialistische Nationalkultur leisten kann. (Franz Fühmann)[1]
> Today's task is to take ownership of the *Nibelungenlied* as heritage. A film could play an outstanding role in this. This would be a contribution only a socialist national culture can make.

How to transform a National Socialist epic into a socialist national epic? In his screenplay *Der Nibelunge Not* (1973), Franz Fühmann (1922–84) boldly attempts to rehabilitate the *Nibelungenlied* for the national canon of the German Democratic Republic after two centuries of misinterpretation and misuse. Fühmann's screenplay was only published posthumously in the GDR in 1987, and remains both unfilmed and notably under-researched in comparison to other aspects of his writing, much of which has itself fallen into obscurity as a result of the large-scale displacement of GDR literature from the post-reunification canon. However, *Der Nibelunge Not* deserves much more attention in critical debates surrounding the reception of classical and medieval epic and the emergence of the concept of a German 'national epic'. In this screenplay, Fühmann radically rejects Enlightenment traditions of reception of the *Nibelungenlied* as 'the German *Iliad*' – and their culmination under National Socialism – in order to rehabilitate the epic as an indispensable element of the 'socialist national culture' of the German Democratic Republic.

---

[1] Fühmann, Franz, 'Szenarium für einen Spielfilm "Das Nibelungenlied"', in Franz Fühmann, *Der Nibelunge Not. Szenarium für einen Spielfilm*, ed. Peter Göhler (Berlin: Aufbau Taschenbuch Verlag, 1993), p. 153 (= *SfeS*). This essay is an adapted extract from a dissertation submitted for the degree of Master of Studies in Modern Languages at the University of Oxford in Trinity Term 2023.

Fühmann's bold claim in the introductory quotation from *Szenarium für einen Spielfilm* – his 1971 film proposal to the DEFA – that the *Nibelungenlied* needed to be reclaimed 'als Erbe überhaupt' (*SfeS*, p. 153) highlights how little engagement with the epic had occurred during the first twenty years of cultural production in the GDR. Just ten versions of the *Nibelungenlied* (and the related Siegfried matter) were produced in the GDR between 1956 and 1971.[2] Four only indirectly drew on the epic via early modern *Volksbücher* – popular versions of highlights from its fairytale and adventure story elements. Three were modern German editions and translations of the epic, including one licensed West German edition. Just three literary texts directly engaged with the *Nibelungenlied* to creatively draw it into GDR national cultural heritage, two of which were Fühmann's own creations – the poem 'Der Nibelunge Not' (1957) and a prose retelling of the epic, *Das Nibelungenlied* (1971). The epic had also largely been relegated from the sphere of national cultural heritage to children's literature and literature for political interest groups. Five of the ten versions were printed by publishers of books for children and young people. What is more, the first ever GDR edition and translation appeared in 1957 with Verlag der Nation – the publisher of the *Nationaldemokratische Partei Deutschlands*, a bloc party for former National Socialists and *Wehrmacht* officers – of which, incidentally, Fühmann had himself been a member between 1950 and 1972. The only adaptations published by more literary publishers were Fühmann's own poem (Aufbau, 1957), two Modern German editions and translations (Reclam, 1961 and Dieterich, 1964), and a Volksbuch edition (Insel, 1969).[3] The scarcity and obscurity of GDR interpretations of the epic before Fühmann's screenplay thus also vindicate his claim that it urgently needed to be more fully integrated into the national cultural heritage of the GDR of the early 1970s.

---

[2]   Grosse, Siegfried and Ursula Rautenberg, *Die Rezeption mittelalterlicher deutscher Dichtung: Eine Bibliographie ihrer Übersetzungen und Bearbeitungen seit der Mitte des 18. Jahrhunderts* (Tübingen: Max Niemeyer Verlag, 1989), pp. 166-230.

[3]   See Hueting, Gail A., 'Book Publishing in the German Democratic Republic', *The Library Quarterly: Information, Community, Policy*, Vol. 52, Nr. 3 (July 1982), pp. 240-59, for more detail on the GDR publishing industry.

Fühmann's sense of urgency to do so reflects wider contemporary concerns surrounding the reappraisal of pre-modern literature and culture and their integration into the national literary and cultural heritage of the GDR against the backdrop of the *Erbediskussion* – an ongoing academic and political debate about the composition and role of national heritage in the GDR. An important example of these emerging reflections in politics is the hardline SED and Kulturbund functionary Hans Koch's (1927-86) article 'Kulturbund und kulturelles Erbe', published in the Kulturbund weekly *Der Sonntag* on 25 May 1975. Koch attempts to make sense of the growing gulf between the rapidly expanding official definition of GDR national heritage and the significantly less rapidly expanding engagement with the often more obscure figures, artefacts and events that had recently been incorporated into it. Koch proposes that this lack of practical engagement is down to a lack of surviving information about the 'wealth of dialectical relationships' between factors such as the objective and subjective reality of historical figures, creators of artefacts and instigators of events, and their status within their 'class', society and wider humanity. He also warns that individual citizens' engagement with GDR national cultural heritage was being weakened by increasingly theoretical and representative official approaches to it. He is concerned that this would weaken ordinary people's ability to engage with it on a practical, everyday level to identify the knowledge and skills that a figure, cultural artefact or event revealed to be essential for individual and collective socialist life and to apply this to their own lives in the present.[4]

Finally, Koch acknowledges that the rapidly expanding definition of cultural heritage increasingly poses the question, 'Wie halten wir es mit der Reaktion?' – the *Gretchenfrage* of GDR cultural heritage – enquiring whether 'reactionary culture' could ever be considered part of 'socialist culture'. Taking the legend of Frederick Barbarossa, he highlights the differences between 'the historical core' and 'the clouds of nationalistic and militaristic stuffiness' surrounding it,

---

[4] Koch, Hans, 'Was, wäre zu fragen, ist unser Erbe?', Peter Lübbe (ed.), *Dokumente zur Kunst-, Literatur- und Kulturpolitik der SED, Band 3: 1975-1980* (Stuttgart: Seewald-Verlag, 1984), pp. 40-41 and 43. All following quotations Koch p. 44.

stressing that much formerly fascist cultural heritage could be integrated into socialist cultural heritage if it underwent 'a great intellectual cleansing'. Explicitly praising Fühmann's 1971 prose retelling of the *Nibelungenlied* as a model of socialist engagement with medieval literature which was once considered 'reactionary', he warns that reluctance to engage with such literary heritage in the GDR risked creating a cultural vacuum which, if not filled by 'progressive' reinterpretations of these texts, would be exploited by the West to openly continue nationalistic and militaristic misuse of them. Concluding that it is impossible to simply write 'the reaction and its further-reaching legacies' out of the canon, he argues that it is imperative for GDR cultural creators to overcome the 'cultural values of hatred and contempt' associated with such works during National Socialism and thereby reclaim these writings for the GDR canon.

Indeed, in contrast to the mere eleven GDR versions of the *Nibelungenlied* and the Siegfried subject matter, a whole 84 versions were produced by the so-called 'reactionary' cultural creators of West Germany before 1973.[5] This total includes 30 children's books and fairytales, 15 editions and translations, 14 narrative or epic retellings, 12 satirical or humorous takes, seven plays, four poems, and two editions of *Volksbuch* versions of the epic – not to mention two film adaptations by Artur Brauner (1966/67) and Adrian Hoven (1970). Although paper shortages and censorship would have been partly responsible for significantly fewer GDR versions of the *Nibelungenlied* having been produced, these factors alone cannot account for this enormous disparity between GDR and FRG editions of the subject matter. Grosse and Rautenberg's bibliography shows that West German writers and cultural figures had begun to re-engage with the *Nibelungenlied* as part of their literary heritage almost a decade earlier than their East German counterparts. They had also engaged with the epic in a more diverse range of genres, including drama, film and parody. Furthermore, they had republished ten earlier re-workings of the epic from 1827 to 1940 in no fewer than sixteen editions, re-

---

[5] This and the following after Grosse / Rautenberg (1989) 166-230.

covering and beginning to engage with editions of the *Nibelungenlied* published prior to the epic's misuse in post-Stalingrad National Socialist 'total war' propaganda which had rendered it culturally unacceptable for a time (see *SfeS*, p. 153), whereas not a single earlier edition had been republished in the GDR.

To overcome such historical baggage resulting from both historical misuse of German cultural heritage and what was perceived as its continuing misuse by Western 'reactionary forces', some East German academics developed new and innovative frameworks for reinterpreting and reclaiming literary texts and other artefacts that were considered important to pre-National Socialist cultural heritage. One contemporary approach which was particularly pertinent to works of medieval literature – especially the *Nibelungenlied* – was proposed by Wolfgang Spiewok (1929-99), Professor of Medieval German in Greifswald, in 1974. From reading Fühmann's own 1971 prose rendering of the *Nibelungenlied* through the lens of contemporary re-evaluations of Vladimir Lenin's cultural theory, Spiewok developed a 'socialist' approach to rehabilitating medieval texts. Spiewok's strategy begins with attaining 'the most historically objective assessment which opens up their true content', which, according to Marxist-Leninist sociology, was only available to the 'proletariat' as the final historical class freed from the concerns of previously dominant socio-economic groups.[6] Spiewok suggests that viewing medieval literature from this proletarian standpoint would enable it to undergo processes of 'party assessment' (*parteiliche Wertung*) which draw out its potential to contribute to the development of socialist individuals and society. Ultimately, Spiewok suggests that attaining a synthesis of this dialectic of objective and partisan interpretation of medieval texts would enable the reader to identify aspects of the text that promoted the 'socialist individual's' intellectual, emotional, moral and ideological development within society, and thus to fulfil the key criteria for admission into the new, 'socialist' national literature of the GDR.

---

[6] This and the following from Spiewok, Wolfgang, 'Zur Erbediskussion aus der Sicht der Mittelalterforschung', *Weimarer Beiträge*, Vol. 20 Nr. 1 (1974), p. 89.

Fühmann's screenplay begins transforming the *Nibelungenlied* into a socialist national epic by separating its subject matter from previous ideological (mis-)appropriations to arrive at the 'most historically objective' interpretation of the epic, qualifying it for recognition as GDR cultural heritage. He begins this process by rejecting the long-established concept of the epic as 'deutsche *Ilias*' (*SfeS*, p. 151), which he ascribes to the historical accident of its rediscovery at the same time as that of classical Homeric poetry in the eighteenth century. He claims that the failure to distinguish between the fundamentally different structures of Homeric and medieval society in the two epics led to Siegfried being misunderstood and misrepresented as a heroic central character *par excellence* (*SfeS*, p. 151), leading to all subsequent interpretations of the epic until National Socialism being skewed towards what he terms 'the reactionary' (*SfeS*, p. 151). To explore how Fühmann counters these 'reactionary' interpretations of the *Nibelungenlied*, Peter Göhler's observation that he presents Siegfried as creating great chaos as a foreign object in the feudal society of his adaptation[7] should be taken further to highlight how Fühmann consistently shows how this disruptive behaviour marks Siegfried out as an 'anachronistisch angelegte Figur' and 'Träger eines nicht-mehr-möglichen Verhaltens' (*SfeS*, p. 151), whose values (idealised by National Socialism) are impossible in modern society.

This notion is symbolically impressed upon the viewer from the beginning through the stage directions describing Siegfried's first appearance on screen: 'Plötzlich sprengt querfeldein eine Schar Reiter der Spitze der Heersäule zu.' (*DNN*, p. 31).[8] Here, Fühmann evokes the highly disruptive nature of Siegfried's character from his very first sudden and unexpected appearance in the world of the epic. In the *Szenarium*, Fühmann reveals how Siegfried cannot sustain his existence in the world of the epic after so violently bursting into it because he thinks in pre-feudal, individualistic categories of 'Abenteuer, Kampf, Jagd, Krieg, Landnahme, Liebe' instead of the more 'feudal',

---

[7] Göhler, Peter, 'Nachwort', *SfeS*, pp. 169-70; cf. also Göhler, Peter, 'Fühmanns Filmentwurf *Der Nibelunge Not*', Paul Alfred Kleinert (ed.), *Filmwelten Franz Fühmanns* (Berlin and Leipzig: Engelsdorfer Verlag, 2022), pp. 77-88, here p. 84.
[8] Franz Fühmann, *Der Nibelunge Not* (= *DNN*) in *SfeS*.

collectivist 'Staatsdenken' (*DNN*, p. 155) which dictates the thinking of all other characters in this world. For instance, Siegfried's conspicuous absence from the meeting of the royal council (*DNN*, pp. 34-36), despite his prominent role in the preceding and subsequent victory celebration scenes, emphasises how he displays no concept of thinking in the interests of the national and international collective, instead consistently thinking in his own interest. A particularly striking example occurs at the end of the first victory ceremony (*DNN*, pp. 32-34). When Gernot and Hagen make the captured kings of Saxony and Denmark kneel in submission before the Burgundian kings, Siegfried reveals that he simply released the king of the Goths because he grew tired of the latter's very bad grace in defeat. Gunther's exasperated comment that Siegfried's prisoner 'war das Haupt des Feindbunds. Nun, da er entkommen ist, wird er es wieder sein!' leads the latter to respond in an even more offhand manner than previously, 'Dann haun wir sie eben nochmals zusammen!' (*DNN*, p. 34).

This response reveals that, instead of thinking in 'feudal' categories of securing the interests of the collective of the state by defeating its enemies and securing peace with other states using astute strategic alliances, he still thinks in pre-feudal terms by seeing these enemies merely as personal adversaries to be crushed using brute force. By describing the way he expresses them as offhand, Fühmann suggests that these categories of Siegfried's thinking are wholly inadequate for the requirements of life in a complex modern society, dissuading the viewer from emulating them. This is compounded by Fühmann's use of the colloquial contracted form 'zusammenhaun' in Siegfried's comment, which is of a much lower register than that typically associated with courtly speech, highlighting at linguistic level how crude and outdated these militaristic ideals (reminiscent of National Socialist thinking) are in the modern world.

Siegfried's archaic status is most aptly reflected by Gere's comment that 'Er zog in Burgund ein wie irgendeiner der Urzeitrecken, von denen die Spielleute auf die Märkte singen!' (*DNN*, p. 35). This reflects traces of more archaic oral traditions associated with Siegfried that recur throughout the courtly poetic structure of the *Nibelungenlied*, such as Hagen's account of Siegfried's battle with the dragon, suggesting the potentially apocryphal nature of his exploits. Here, the simile describing Siegfried's entry into Burgundy underlines how outdated the frameworks which govern his behaviour are by associating them with an undefined, primal period which is so pre-historical as to be extra-historical. The other highly archaic term, 'Recke', in this compound noun also reinforces just how out-of-place Siegfried is by echoing the different linguistic levels of the *Nibelungenlied* which distinguish characters associated with historic Germanic heroic ideals from those associated with contemporary ideals of French courtly culture. The most ancient connotations of this word, associating Siegfried with the giants of ancient Germanic legend, denote him as a grotesque character whose attitudes and behaviour sharply contrast with those expected of a character in his position in medieval society. The term's further Old High German connotations of a 'hero driven out of his homeland'[9] also emphasise how Siegfried very clearly belongs to a different geographical and temporal homeland to the world of the screenplay. In addition to diminishing Siegfried's esteem in the eyes of the viewer by revealing Gere's highly dismissive attitude towards him, Fühmann's use of the indefinite pronoun 'irgendeiner' to qualify this compound noun reinforces the sense of defamiliarisation that he attaches to Siegfried throughout the screenplay. In these episodes, Fühmann therefore separates the epic from eighteenth-century German nationalist interpretations of it by differentiating between the social frameworks that govern the behaviour of pre-feudal and feudal characters, highlighting how Siegfried's 'reactionary', individualistic values and attitudes are unsustainable in modern societies much more oriented towards the needs and values of collectives of class, nation and the world at large.

---

[9] *Deutsches Wörterbuch von Jacob Grimm und Wilhelm Grimm* (= *DWB*), digitalisierte Fassung im Wörterbuchnetz des Trier Center for Digital Humanities, Version 01/23, vol. 14 (1887), 'recke, m.', www.woerterbuchnetz.de/DWB/recke.

Throughout the screenplay, Fühmann starkly contrasts the militaristic and inhumane qualities that he associates with 'pre-feudal' characters such as Siegfried with the more 'feudal' layers of the epic that he interprets as moving closer to the ideals of 'socialist culture' of the East German nation. This was defined by the 1968 GDR constitution as rooted in peace, humanism and international co-operation and actively opposing 'imperialist un-culture' rooted in warfare, cruelty and rivalrous nationalism.[10] An example of how Fühmann reinterprets the *Nibelungenlied* as a literary text that works against the glorification of violence to promote peace can be seen when the crowd falls silent after Gunther's angry retort to Siegfried that Burgundy's power was not built on daring and boldness, adding emphasis to his critique of Siegfried's militarism. In response to this silence, Gunther stands together with the defeated kings and proclaims that 'Versöhnung ist der Wille Burgunds!' and 'ruft ins Volk: Versöhnung! Frieden!', which the people jubilantly acclaim (*DNN*, p. 34). Fühmann's contrast between Siegfried's boldness and Gunther's irenic disposition reveals his rejection of Siegfried's warlike ideals in favour of new ideals of reconciliation and peace that look ahead to ideals of socialist internationalism, with which Fühmann encourages the audience to identify through the final stage direction in this scene highlighting the acclaim that this action receives from the ordinary people assembled there.

Fühmann also seeks to rehabilitate the *Nibelungenlied* by suggesting how it promotes Marxist ideals of 'socialist humanism', the essence of which is defined by Michael Kinne and Birgit Strube-Edelmann as 'elimination of all exploitation and oppression of the human being' which would be 'fully realised' 'in socialist and communist society'.[11] These humanist ideals of non-exploitation and non-oppression that Fühmann presents in *Der Nibelunge Not* can be observed in Fühmann's presentation of the Burgundian kings' respect for the human

---

[10] *Verfassung der Deutschen Demokratischen Republik vom 9. April 1968*, Artikel 18, https://www.verfassungen.de/ddr/verf68-i.htm.

[11] Kinne, Michael and Strube-Edelmann, Birgit, 'Sozialistischer Humanismus', in: Michael Kinne, Birgit Strube-Edelmann (edd.), *Kleines Wörterbuch des DDR-Wortschatzes* (Düsseldorf: Pädagogischer Verlag, 2nd edn. 1981), p. 185.

dignity of their captured Saxon and Danish counterparts. Before the defeated kings appear, two wounded knights from each army are brought on in 'zwei gepolsterten Wagen', which are 'ehrenvoll links und rechts neben den Thronen aufgestellt' (both *DNN*, p. 32). Here, Fühmann presents the Burgundians' dignified treatment of these wounded prisoners of war as a 'feudal' ancestor of these ideals of socialist humanism. Instead of being treated like objects and spoils of war, they are treated with the decency that human beings deserve, transported in comfort and treated with the same dignity afforded to the victors by remaining directly beside their thrones throughout the scene. This is reinforced by Fühmann's stage directions associated with the homage paid by the defeated king of Denmark, which stress that the scenes are to take place 'mit der höchsten Würde und keinesfalls mit Brutalität oder mit kleinlicher Schikane und Kränkung gegenüber den Gefangenen' (*DNN*, p. 33). This highly humane and dignified treatment of prisoners starkly contrasts with Siegfried's shockingly gratuitous violence against the defeated Wild Man: 'Siegfried lifts the wild man up high and smashes him onto the floorboards. The wild man's ribs shatter; blood gushes from his nose. Siegfried laughs as he places his foot on his neck' (*DNN*, p. 38), further discrediting Siegfried and the 'cultural values of hatred and contempt' associated with him by showing just how far removed the ideals he embodies are from those of the 'socialist' values of human dignity on which the GDR professed to be founded.

In addition, Fühmann clearly distances the *Nibelungenlied* from National Socialist misappropriations of it, which he suggests largely proceed from Enlightenment misinterpretations of Siegfried combined with *Gründerzeit* reworkings of it as a foundational epic for the new German Empire praising the ancient 'Germanic' values on which this new nation-state and society were purportedly founded. Werner Wunderlich's observation that Fühmann's screenplay, like his eponymous poem, is 'concerned with coming to terms with the Third Reich and the purposes to which it used the epic'[12] should be

---

[12] Wunderlich, Werner, 'Fühmann, Franz', in: Francis G. Gentry, Winder McConnell, Ulrich Müller, Werner Wunderlich (edd.), *The Nibelungen Tradition: An Encyclopedia* (New York/London: Routledge, 2002), p. 239.

taken further to investigate how Fühmann's screenplay actively works against the lingering influence of National Socialist appropriation of the epic. For instance, Fühmann's screenplay expressly works against National Socialist use of the *Nibelungenlied* in the final years of the Second World War to promote the ideal of a nation-state founded on absolute individual obedience to the supreme authority figures under even the most hopeless of circumstances (*SfeS*, p. 153). Fühmann's characterisation of this misinterpretation as the 'Nach-Stalingrad-Phase' in National Socialist reception of the epic refers to Hermann Göring's January 1943 speech in which he likened the hopelessly outnumbered German troops in Stalingrad to the Nibelungs' 'Kampf ohnegleichen' to the last man in the burning banqueting hall.[13] In the screenplay, Fühmann comprehensively distances this episode from Göring's infamous misappropriation of it by declining to depict the events in the burning banqueting hall at all. Instead, the viewer only sees their aftermath before the final battle: 'der Innenhof vor dem ausgebrannten, noch qualmenden Festsaal. Der Hof liegt voller Leichname, umgekommen durchs Schwert wie durchs Feuer. Die ausgebrannte Halle scheint leer' (*DNN*, p. 135). It is also striking that Fühmann uses animated rather than live-action footage in his depiction of this battle, which clearly distances this episode from the live-action scenes surrounding it and presents it in an ironic light by subtly suggesting that it may be a fictional invention. Additionally, Fühmann's stage direction 'Wie klein diese Menschlein doch erscheinen!', and the emphasis that he places on the Burgundians' 'Marionettenhaftigkeit' (both *DNN*, p. 135), ironically distances this episode from Göring's perverse parallel between the Wehrmacht and the Nibelungs by deflating the heroic status that Göring ascribed to the combatants. Furthermore, Fühmann's description of the final battle as a 'kurzes Getümmel' (*DNN*, p. 135) during which Volker and Gernot are slain before Hagen and Gunther are overpowered mocks Göring's presentation of this episode as an unparalleled heroic fight to the last man. This is underlined by the term *Getümmel*'s status

---

[13]   Hermann Goering's speech of 18 January 1943, in Dietrich Möller, 'Geschichte aktuell' (18 November 2002), (accessed 11/05/2024).

as 'auszerordentlich beliebt [...] für kampf- und schlachtszenen', reflected by the long list of examples of its usage in this sense from Luther to Hebbel.[14] Fühmann's concerted efforts outlined above to shift the battle into a lower register make it appear much less uniquely elevated than National Socialist interpretations of it suggest and thus distance this episode from National Socialist misuse of it to promote ideologies which idealised war and violence.

Furthermore, Fühmann assumes a clear distance from earlier, underlying National Socialist misappropriations of the *Nibelungenlied* as a 'national epic' promoting the ideal of an ethnically and linguistically homogeneous Germanic nation-state and lamenting the 'betrayal' of idealised 'Nordic' characters such as Siegfried by 'ethnically inferior' 'Dinaric' characters such as Hagen by explicitly confronting National Socialist use of these terms in relation to the epic (*SfeS*, p. 153). In the screenplay, Fühmann confounds this National Socialist racial binary with an ethnically and linguistically diverse cast of characters, which, he states in his film proposal, will need to be reflected by an equally diverse casting of actors, stressing that the Huns and Icelanders – especially Brunhild – should be played by non-German actors (*SfeS*, p. 161). Incidentally, throughout the film, Fühmann spells Brünhild's name as 'Brynhild', drawing her closer to her incarnation as 'Brynhildr' in the Icelandic Edda cycle and working against National Socialist attempts to easily familiarise and appropriate her as a 'German' character.

Fühmann's insistence that the Huns should be played by non-Germans also distances them from National Socialist portrayals of them as sub-human by typecasting them for a sense of foreignness which embodied 'the very prototype of the barbarian'.[15] Fühmann achieves this by no longer presenting them as jabbering away in 'incomprehensible language' as they do in Fritz Lang's 1924 film adaptation,

---

[14] DWB 6 (1898) s.v. www.woerterbuchnetz.de/DWB/getümmel.
[15] Brüggen, Elke and Holznagel, Franz-Josef, '*Des künic Etzelen man*: The Huns and their King in Fritz Lang's Classic Silent Film Die Nibelungen and in the Nibelungenlied', *Thamyris/Intersecting*, Nr. 29 (2015), p. 223.

instead providing them with distinctive voices which create linguistic diversity in the script and force the viewer to assume a critical distance to their preconceptions of the epic. For example, the stage directions in I,2 state that 'Einer der Hunnen wendet sich *in hunnischer Sprache* an Rüdiger und fragt, ob das vor ihnen Worms sei, ein ungewohntes Wort, das ihm schwer über die Zunge geht.' (*DNN*, p. 12; my emphasis). The unusual sound of the German place name 'Worms' when the Hunnish rider attempts to pronounce it creates defamiliarisation through placing aural distance between the German-speaking viewer and an otherwise familiar place name. This defamiliarisation is further reinforced by the stage direction, 'Wir blicken mit den hunnischen Edlen auf die Stadt' (*DNN*, p. 12), which forces the viewer to view the film's familiar German setting from a non-German perspective. Furthermore, Rüdiger's reply to the Hun in Hunnish is particularly striking because it reveals him to be a much less unequivocally 'German' character than previous nationalist representations of him seemed to suggest. According to Grosse and Rautenberg, the character of Rüdiger had inspired eight spin-off tragedies between 1849 and 1939, including Felix Dahn's *Markgraf Rüdeger von Bechelaren* (1875) and the 1939 drama *Rüdiger von Bechelaren* by Hans Baumann, a National Socialist now best known for composing the German Labour Front anthem. Although it is unclear whether Fühmann was aware of these specific dramas, both authors' ideologically problematic historical novels had previously enjoyed huge popularity. Fühmann's conscious presentation of Rüdiger as transcending the divide between 'German' and 'Hun' thus most likely works against broader nationalist appropriation of the epic by such well-known earlier authors. Moreover, it is significant that the first words spoken in the film are not in German; instead, they form the end of the Latin *Gloria in excelsis deo* (*SfeS*, p. 11) – the international *lingua franca* of what Ernst Robert Curtius termed the 'Latin Middle Ages'. This has the effect of lifting the screenplay's plot out of the exclusively German context in which previous nationalist versions had presented it and recontextualising it within the broader framework of thirteenth-century Central European society.

Fühmann's consistent emphasis on the internationality and diversity of the *Nibelungenlied* thus underlines the 'räumliche Weite' of the epic, countering aggressively nationalist Third Reich versions with a version which reflects the 'international character of socialist ideology'[16] and justifies its reintegration into GDR cultural heritage. This superseding of the inward-looking nationalisms previously associated with the *Nibelungenlied* is most clearly exemplified by Fühmann's presentation of Etzel's kingdom, a multi-ethnic state which brings together 'Herren und Damen aller Hautfarben und Rassenphysiognomien; es kann auf der Welt keine Gala und keine – weltlichen wie geistlichen – Würdenzeichen geben, die hier nicht vertreten wären' (*DNN*, p. 105). In the *Szenarium für einen Spielfilm*, Fühmann describes his presentation of Etzel's kingdom as an ideal higher order bringing together many different peoples in a spirit of tolerance and peace 'in der sich eine Einheit von ritterlicher Ethik und Staatsmacht verkörpert' (SfeS, p. 159). The 'unity' that Fühmann evokes as the lasting impression of Etzel's kingdom at the end of this section of his film proposal reveals that such a structure of society would enable a synthesis of the dialectic between the 'ethical imperatives' governing individuals' personal conduct and the 'power of the state' governing public and political conduct (*SfeS*, p. 159). He suggests that this would enable its citizens to become successful classconscious citizens (*SfeS*, p. 159) – provided that its leaders were experienced in resisting intrigues and its army were strong enough to defend it from warlike enemies (*SfeS*, p. 159) – clearly establishing this apparently utopian situation as something to be worked towards which can be realised under the right social and political conditions.

Der Nibelunge Not thus represents a radical rejection of existing concepts of the *Nibelungenlied* as a foundational epic on the level of the *Iliad* for the German nation. In the screenplay, Fühmann pursues an innovative approach to recovering the *Nibelungenlied* from its comparative obscurity in the GDR against the backdrop of contemporary debates surrounding what constituted the foundation of cultural heritage for the East German state and the role that this heritage should

---

[16] Spiewok, 'Zur Erbediskussion', p. 91.

play in the everyday life of the nation. He parses apart the pre-feudal / heroic and feudal / courtly layers of the epic, revealing just how anachronistic he perceives the individualistic behaviour of Siegfried to be within a structure of society that increasingly favours the collective over the individual. He also works against National Socialist appropriation of the epic which promoted a form of nationalism based on militaristic violence, racist notions of ethnic homogeneity, and blind, suicidal loyalty to supreme leaders governing the state. Instead, he suggests how this epic could be rehabilitated and reintegrated into the cultural heritage of the GDR to promote peace, human dignity, and co-operation between social groups to establish a collective founded on these values. In this way, as Peter Göhler suggests, Fühmann's adaptation of *Der Nibelunge Not* makes the epic 'untauglich […] für seine Einvernahme für Gewalt und schauerliche Verherrlichung von Totschlag, Mord und Krieg'[17] for which it had been misused as a foundational text by nationalists and National Socialists alike.

---

[17] Göhler, Peter, 'Fühmanns Filmentwurf Der Nibelunge Not', Paul Alfred Kleinert (ed.), Franz Fühmanns Filmwelten (Leipzig: Engelsdorfer Verlag, 2022), p. 87.

Appendix: Epic Beginnings

The quotations are sorted in chronological order, based mainly on books chosen for the exhibition; in brackets the catalogue sections.

Iliad

μῆνιν ἄειδε θεὰ Πηληϊάδεω Ἀχιλῆος
οὐλομένην, ἣ μυρί' Ἀχαιοῖς ἄλγε' ἔθηκε,
πολλὰς δ' ἰφθίμους ψυχὰς Ἄϊδι προΐαψεν
ἡρώων, αὐτοὺς δὲ ἑλώρια τεῦχε κύνεσσιν
οἰωνοῖσί τε πᾶσι, Διὸς δ' ἐτελείετο βουλή,
ἐξ οὗ δὴ τὰ πρῶτα διαστήτην ἐρίσαντε
Ἀτρεΐδης τε ἄναξ ἀνδρῶν καὶ δῖος Ἀχιλλεύς.

Homeri Opera in five vols, OUP 1920
online as part of the Perseus Project.

Sing, o göttliche singe den zorn des Peliden, der unheil
Ueber die Griechen gehäuft, die helden zum Orcus gesendet,
Und die körper zum aas den hunden und vögeln gegeben;
Dadnrch [!] wurde der willen des obersten Gottes erfüllet,
Als Achilles und Agamemnon, der könig der schaaren,
Streit gewannen und zwietracht der beiden herzen zertrennte.

Bodmer 1767 (section 1), p. 159.

Singe den Zorn, o Göttin, des Peleiaden Achilleus,
Ihn, der entbrannt den Achaiern unnennbaren Jammer erregte,
Und viel tapfere Seelen der Heldensöhne zum Ais
Sendete, aber sie selber zum Raub' ausstreckte den Hunden,
Und dem Gevögel umher: so ward Zeus Wille vollendet:
Seit dem Tag', als einst durch bitteren Zank sich entzweiten
Atreus Sohn, der Herrscher des Volks, und der edle Achilleus.

Voß 1844 (section 3), vol. 1, p. 3.

Of Peleus' son, Achilles, sing, O Muse,
The vengeance, deep and deadly; whence to Greece
Unnumber'd ills arose; which many a soul
Of mighty warriors to the viewless shades

Untimely sent; they on the battle plain
Unburied lay, a prey to rav'ning dogs,
And carrion birds; but so Heav'n decreed,
From that sad day when first in wordy war,
The mighty Agamemnon, king of men,
Confronted stood by Peleus' godlike son.
> Lord Stanley 1862 (section 2), p. 1.

In uralten Zeiten wohnten auf der Insel Samothrace, im ägäischen Meere, zwei Brüder, Jasion und Dardanus, Söhne des Jupiter und einer Nymphe, Fürsten des Landes.
> Schwab 1882 (section 3), beginning of 'Die Sagen Troja's'.

Sing, o Göttin, von Zorn, von des Peleussohnes Achilleus
Heillosem Zorn, der unsägliches Leid den Achäern gestiftet,
Der viel tapfere Seelen zu Hades niedergesendet,
Seelen der Helden, indes er sie selber den Hunden zum Raube
Schuf und den Vögeln zum Frass, – so gieng Zeus Rat in Erfüllung,
Seit dem Tag, da zuerst sich die Beiden in Hader entzweiten
Atreus Sohn, der Gebieter des Heers und der hehre Achilleus.
> Fick 1902 (section 2), p. 1.

In der Odyssee habe ich euch erzählt, daß die Griechen in den Krieg nach Troja mußten, weil Paris dem König Menelaos die Frau geraubt hatte. Ein Stück von dem Kriege will ich euch nun erzählen. Die Griechen hatten schon lange um Troja gekämpft. Mal hatten die Griechen gesiegt und mal die Troer. Aber die Griechen hatten Troja nicht zerstören können, denn soweit waren sie nie gekommen. Deswegen war der Krieg noch immer nicht zu Ende.
> Otto 1904 (section 5), p. 1.

In the deep forest that clothes Mound Ida, not far from the strong city of Troy, Paris, son of King Priam, watched his father's flocks by night.
> Lang n.d. (section 5), p. 1.

Once upon a time there was a certain King of Sparta who had a most beautiful daughter, Helen by name. There was not a prince in Greece but wished to marry her.
> Church 1908 (section 6), p. 15.

Singe, Göttin, den Zorn des Peleiaden Achilleus,
Der zum Verhängnis unendliche Leiden schuf den Achaiern
Und die Seelen so vieler gewaltiger Helden zum Hades
Sandte, aber sie selbst zum Raub den Hunden gewährte
Und den Vögeln zum Fraß – so wurde der Wille Kronions
Endlich erfüllt –, nachdem sich einmal im Zwiste geschieden
Atreus' Sohn, der Herrscher des Volks, und der edle Achilleus.

> Voß/Rupé 1922 (section 2), p. 1.

To the ancient Greeks the Siege of Troy was the greatest and most important event in the Age of Heroes – that age of wonder when the Immortals who dwelt on Olympus and whom they worshipped as gods, mingled with mankind and took a visible part in their affairs.

> Green 1965 (section 5), p. 10.

Singe uns, Göttin, vom Zorn des Peleus-Sohnes Achilleus,
Der unendliches Leid hat den Achaiern gebracht.
Vieler Helden Seelen hat er zum Hades gesendet,
Während er ihren Leib Hunden und Vögeln zum Fraß
Liegen ließ, daß sich erfüllte der Wille des Vaters der Götter.
Denn in schrecklichem Zwist hatten sich bitter entzweit
Atreus' Sohn, der Beherrscher des Volks, und der edle Achilleus.

> Hoepke 1977 (section 5), p. 9.

In a small kingdom in the north of Greece ruled Peleus, king of Phthia, who was much favoured by the gods. When he was no longer young, he fell in love with the sea-goddess Thetis, daughter of blue-haired and blue-bearded Nereus, who dwelt in the depths of the Aegean Sea, together with his consort, Doris, and their fifty daughters.

> Picard 1986 (section 5), p. 1.

This is the story of a bitter quarrel between two proud and powerful men. It brought death to hundreds of brave heroes and destroyed one of the great cities of the world. And yet it started with something very small ... It all began with an apple.

> Cross 2012 (section 4), p. 11.

Now that I'm dead I know everything. This is what I wished would happen, but like so many of my wishes it failed to come true. I know only a few factoids that I didn't know before. Death is much too high a price to pay for the satisfaction of curiosity, needless to say.

    Atwood 2018 (section 6), p. 1.

Troy. The most marvellous kingdom in all the world. The Jewel of the Aegean. Glittering Ilium, the city that rose and fell not once but twice. Gatekeeper of traffic in and out of the barbarous east. Kingdom of gold and horses. Fierce nurse of prophets, princes, heroes, warriors and poets. Under the protection of ARES, ARTEMIS, APOLLO and APHRODITE she stood for years as the paragon of all that can be achieved in the arts of war and peace, trade and treaty, love and art, statecraft, piety and civil harmony. When she fell, a hole opened in the human world that may never be filled, save in memory. Poets must sing the story over and over again, passing it from generation to generation, lest in losing Troy we lose a part of ourselves.

    Fry 2020 (section 3), p. 1.

Odyssey

ἄνδρα μοι ἔννεπε, μοῦσα, πολύτροπον, ὃς μάλα πολλὰ
πλάγχθη, ἐπεὶ Τροίης ἱερὸν πτολίεθρον ἔπερσεν·
πολλῶν δ' ἀνθρώπων ἴδεν ἄστεα καὶ νόον ἔγνω,
πολλὰ δ' ὅ γ' ἐν πόντῳ πάθεν ἄλγεα ὃν κατὰ θυμόν,
ἀρνύμενος ἥν τε ψυχὴν καὶ νόστον ἑταίρων.

Homer, *Odyssey*, ed. by William Heinemann 1919
online as part of the Perseus Project.

Sage mir, Muse, die Thaten des vielgewanderten Mannes,
Welcher so weit geirrt, nach der heiligen Troja Zerstörung,
Vieler Menschen Städte gesehn, und Sitte gelernt hat,
Und auf dem Meere so viel' unnennbare Leiden erduldet,
Seine Seele zu retten, und seiner Freunde Zurückkunft.
Aber die Freunde rettet' er nicht, wie eifrig er strebte;
Denn sie bereiteten selbst durch Missethat ihr Verderben:
Thoren! welche die Rinder des hohen Sonnenbeherschers
Schlachteten; siehe, der Gott nahm ihnen den Tag der Zurückkunft.
Sage hievon auch uns ein weniges, Tochter Kronions.

    Voß 1781 (section 2), p. 9.

Melde den Mann mir, Muse, den Vielgewandten, der vielfach
Umgeirrt, als Troja, die heilige Stadt, er zerstöret;
Vieler Menschen Städte gesehn, und Sitte gelernt hat,
Auch im Meere so viel herzkrankende Leiden erduldet,
Strebend für seine Seele zugleich und der Freunde Zurückkunft.
Nicht die Freunde jedoch errettet' er, eifrig bemüht zwar;
Denn sie bereiteten selbst durch Missethat ihr Verderben:
Thörichte, welche die Rinder dem leuchtenden Sohn Hyperions
Schlachteten; jener darauf nahm ihnen den Tag der Zurückkunft.
Hievon sag' auch uns ein Weniges, Tochter Kronions.

    Voß 1844 (section 3), vol. 2, p. 1.

Odysseus war der Sohn des Laertes und König von Ithaka. Er war weit berühmt wegen seiner Klugheit und Tapferkeit. Er war auch schon verheiratet und hatte einen kleinen Sohn, den Telemach. Da mußten plötzlich alle Griechen in den Krieg. Paris, der Sohn des Königs Priamos, hatte die Frau des Königs Menelaos geraubt. Die war das schönste Weib bei den Menschen. Sie hieß Helena. Menelaos wollte seine Frau natürlich wieder haben und bat nun die anderen Griechen, ihm zu helfen. Sie wollten das gern, denn wer hilft wohl nicht gern seinen Nachbarn?

> Otto 1903 (section 4), p. 1.

In the days of long ago there reigned over Ithaca, a rugged little island in the sea to the west of Greece, a king whose name was Odysseus. Odysseus feared no man. Stronger and braver than other men was he, wiser, and more full of clever devices. Far and wide he was known as Odysseus of the many counsels. Wise, also, was his queen, Penelope, and she was as fair as she was wise; and as good as she was fair.

> Lang n.d. (section 4), p. 1.

A great many years ago there was a very famous siege of a city called Troy.

> Church 1907 (section 6), p. 15.

This is the story of Odysseus, the most renowned of all the heroes the Greek poets have told us of – of Odysseus, his wars and wanderings. And this story of Odysseus begins with his son, the youth who was called Telemachus.

> Colum 1920 (section 6), p. 3.

This history tells of the wanderings of Ulysses and his followers in their return from Troy, after the destruction of that famous city of Asia by the Grecians. He was inflamed with desire of seeing again, after ten years' absence, his wife and native country Ithaca.

> Lamb 1926 (section 4), p. 7.

Muse, erzähle uns von jenem gewaltigen Helden,
Der die Stadt Troja zerstört, der dann irrte umher,
Viele Menschen und Städte sah, auf Wogen des Meeres
Schmerzen und Leiden ertrug! Immer war er besorgt
Um das eigene Leben und um die Heimkehr der Freunde.
War er auch noch so bemüht – dennoch gelang's ihm nicht.
Denn sie gingen zugrunde durch ihren eigenen Frevel.
Rinder des Helios hatten sie umgebracht.
Deshalb versagte der zornige Gott die Stunde der Heimkehr.
Davon erzähle uns, Muse, soviel Du weißt!

> Hoepke 1975 (section 4), p. 11.

Appendix

After their ten-year-long war with the men of Troy was ended and the Trojan city had fallen in flames and smoke, the victorious Greeks gathered together their booty and their prisoners; and when the great King Agamemnon, who was in charge of all the Grecian host, had given the word, one by one all those leaders of the Greeks who had survived the fighting boarded their ships and set sail for home.

Picard 1986 (section 5), p. 215.

Nibelungenlied

Uns ist in alten mæren wunders vil geseit
von helden lobebæren, von grôzer arebeit,
von freuden hôchgezîten, von weinen und von klagen,
von küener recken strîten muget ir nû wunder hœren sagen.
> *Das Nibelungenlied*, ed. Karl Bartsch 1866
> on google books from Taylorian Vet.Ger.III.B.552.
> On display: Ed. Bartsch/de Boor 1988 (section 3), p. 3.

Eh die aonischen Musen in Deutschlands hainen gewandelt,
Als Achilles noch nicht in deutschen gesängen gefochten,
Und Ulysses die freyer noch nicht im bettler betrogen,
Sangen die Eschilbache, von deutschen Musen begeistert,
Eigne gesänge, die frucht des selbst erfindenden geistes.
Einer von ihnen sang mit Mäonides tone die schwester,
Welcher die brüder den theuen [sic] gemahl erschlugen, die schwester
Wieder die brüder erschlug. Die zeit hat den nahmen getilget,
Aber sein lied gerettet, ich hab' es gehört, und ich will es
Lauter singen, es soll vom Rhein zur Ostsee ertönen.
> Bodmer 1767 (section 1), p. 309.

In ancient song and story marvels high are told,
Of knights of high emprize, and adventures manifold;
Of joy and merry feasting; of lamenting, woe, and fear;
Of champions' bloody battles many marvels shall ye hear.
> *Illustrations of Northern Antiquities, From the Earlier Teuronic and Scandinavian Romances; Being an Abstract of the Book of Heroes and Nibelungen Lay* […], [ed. by H. W. Weber, R. Jamieson, and Sir W. Scott.] Edinburgh 1814, p. 167.

Uns ist in alten Mären des Wunders viel gesagt
Von Helden, reich an Ehren, in Mühsal unverzagt.
Von Freude und Festzeiten, von Weinen und von Klagen,
Von kühner Recken Streiten mögt ihr nun Wunder hören sagen.
> Marbach 1840 (section 5), n. pag.

Uns ist in alten Mären Wunders viel gesait
Von Helden, werth der Ehren, von großer Kühnheit;

48 *Appendix*

Von Freuden und Hochgezeiten, von Weinen und von Klagen,
Von kühner Recken Streiten mögt Ihr nun Wunder hören sagen.
> Pfizer 1843 (section 4), p. 1.

Legends of bygone times reveal wonders and prodigies,
Of heroes worthy endless fame, – of matchless braveries, –
Of jubilees and festal sports, – of tears and sorrows great, –
And knights who daring combats fought: the like I now relate.
> *Das Nibelungen Lied; or, Lay of the Last Nibelungers*, translated into English verse after Carl Lachmann's collated and corrected text by Jonathan Birch, Berlin 1848, p. 1

The Lay of the Nibelungen princes! What is it? A strange, wild story, full of weird beauty and god-like heroism, like the gleams of light in a Salvator landscape, with a background of storm and darkness. The old, old story of woman's passionate love, and impulsive forgetfulness of consequences; of man's protecting tenderness and chivalrous daring; but true knight and queenly woman alike falling victims to the bad man, with the indomitable will, who comes before us as a grotesque mockery of humanity, endowed with all subtlety of intellect, but having a fossilized heart.
> Hands 1880 (section 6), p. 1.

In old tales they tell us many wonders of heroes and of high courage, of glad feasting, of wine and of mourning; and herein ye shall read of the marvellous deeds and of the strife of brave men.
> Armour 1897 (section 6), p. 1.

Long, long ago, in the kingdom of Burgundy, there lived a princess named Kriemhilda, whose beauty, gentleness, and virtue were famed throughout the land. Her father had died during her early maidenhood, and since that unhappy day she had resided with her mother under the safe protection of her three brothers – Gunther, Gernot, and Giselher.
> Anon. 1907 (section 4), p. 9.

Siegfried was born a Prince and grew to be a hero, a hero with a heart of gold. Though he could fight, and was as strong as any lion, yet he could love too and be as gentle as a child.
> MacGregor 1908 (section 4), p. 1.

Long ago, comrades, brave things were seen in this city. For the old king, whom men called Dankrat, had driven back his enemies, as the wind scatters the thunder-clouds; and now in his old age he lived rich and in peace wirh his noble wife Uté, his little daughter Kriemhild, and his three sons.

> Anon. 1911 (section 6), p. 7.

Siegfried was a great and noble prince whose fame, by reason of his mighty deeds, hath endurance through the Ages. His sire was King Siegmund of the Netherlands and his mother was named Sigelinde. Ere yet he had reached the years that are mellowed by wisdom, Siegfried was of proud and haughty spirit and brooked not restraint. Great was his strength, and if his playfellows obeyed not his will in all things, he smote them harshly, so that the hated as much as they feared him. Wild and wilful was the prince as a lad may be.

> Mackenzie 1912 (section 6), p. 354.

Im Burgunderlande wuchs ein edles Mädchen auf, es mochte wohl im ganzen Lande kein schöneres geben. Kriemhild hieß sie und gedieh zu einem herrlichen Weibe, um das dereinst viele edle Helden ihr Leben verlieren sollten. Sie war im ganzen Lande beliebt, und ihre keusche Sitte galt allen Frauen zum Vorbilde. Drei reiche, mächtige Fürsten, Gunther, Gernot und Giselher, welches ihre Brüder waren, betreuten sie.

> Wägner/Heichen 1943 (section 5), p. 83.

Viel Staunenswertes ist in den alten Geschichten auf uns gekommen: Kunde von hochberühmten Helden und ihren Taten und ihrer Not, von Festesfreuden und Jammergeschrei und den Kämpfen der Kühnen, und wer mag, kann nun von all dem hören, es werden aber wundersame Dinge darunter sein.

> Fühmann 2005 (section 3), p. 6.

fliederung dunkler fluff – tüpfel
sehe schuss siena gebrannt um flügel
karmin karneol spüre herzschlag siena
flirres gespan klöppel der schwinge
luftwärts gebannt unter eines körpers
flitsch
 – fahre auf

> Draesner 2016 (section 4), p. 5.

Exhibition Catalogues

Taylorian: Epic! Homer and the *Nibelungenlied* in Translation curated by MARY BOYLE and PHILIP FLACKE

1. Epic?

Illustration 11: Section 1. From top to bottom, left to right: Bodmer 1767, Schultz 1901, Stolte 1877, Fenik 1986. Photograph: Philip Flacke

'Dieses Gedicht hat etwas iliadisches' – 'There is something *Iliad*-like about this poem'. With these words, in 1757, the Swiss critic Johann Jakob Bodmer set the tone for public perceptions of the *Nibelungenlied* for years to come. The thirteenth-century German epic had been rediscovered just two years earlier, and Bodmer was its first editor, though he only printed a section of the text. In the course of his work, he thoroughly reshaped the material according to his own theories on epic. This was informed by his collaboration with Johann Jakob Breitinger, in which the two men had already laid the groundwork for a new understanding of Homer, focusing less on authoritative rules than on supposed original 'genius'. The mid-eighteenth century thus marks the starting point for a shared reception of both Homer and the *Nibelungenlied*.

Reading, translating, and adapting either text has often meant invoking the other. Not only has the *Nibelungenlied* been adapted in the metre of Homer, the hexameter, but Homer, too, has been translated in ways that imitate the form of the *Nibelungenlied*. Labelling the story of Siegfried and Kriemhild a 'German *Iliad*' became a trope, and not just in the German-speaking world, but in the anglophone world as well. When William Morris wrote of 'the Great Story of the North, which should be to all our race what the Tale of Troy was to the Greeks', he was referring primarily to the Old Norse *Völsunga Saga*, but this was often incorporated into English-language retellings of the *Nibelungenlied*, particularly where it was felt that there were gaps in the narrative. The supposed connection between the Nibelungen material and Homer also reached the United States where, in 1892, a school reader entitled *The Story of the German Iliad*, taught sixth- and seventh-grade students about the 'Rhine-gold', Siegfried's death and Kriemhilda's revenge.

In the academic world, Homer and the *Nibelungenlied* have sometimes been the subject of comparative study to this day. This got its second wind, when in the 1930s, the American Classicist Milman Parry and his pupil Albert B. Lord developed their theories on the specifics of so-called 'oral poetry'. They had studied the living tradition of Serbo-Croatian *guslars* in order to better understand the development and transmission of the Homeric epics. But their findings have since also been linked to the *Nibelungenlied*.

1757 *Chriemhilden Rache, und Die Klage; Zwey Heldengedichte. Aus dem schvväbischen Zeitpuncte samt Fragmenten aus dem Gedichte von den Nibelungen und aus dem Josaphat*, [ed. by Johann Jacob Bodmer], Zürich.
Taylor Institution Library: ARCH.8o.G.1757

In the first modern edition of the *Nibelungenlied*, the text has undergone major changes. Bodmer cut about two thirds, presenting only the last part with the Burgundians at the court of Kriemhild's second husband Etzel and Kriemhild's revenge for the death of Siegfried together with 'fragments' from the first two thirds. This drastic interference with the text is part of an attempt to make it more like the *Iliad*.

> All these passages I have cut out and, I believe, with the same legitimacy as Homer when he left out Helen's abduction, Iphigenia's sacrifice, and all the events of the ten years preceding the dispute between Achilles and Agamemnon, to which he only refers on occasion as to something generally known.
>
> (Alle diese Stücke habe ich abgeschnitten, und ich glaube mit demselben Rechte, mit welchem Homer die Entführung der Helena, die Aufopferung der Iphigenia, und alle Begegnisse der zehn Jahre, die vor dem Zwiste zwischen Achilles und Agamemnon vorhergegangen sind, weggelassen hat, auf die er nur bey Gelegenheiten sich als auf bekannte Sachen beziehet.)

Other aspects in which the *Nibelungenlied* resembles Homer according to Bodmer include the different facets of bravery in various heroes, the variety of battle scenes, and the immediacy with which the poet immerses his audience in the action. As to the first two thirds of the *Nibelungenlied*, Bodmer sees 'no indication that it will ever be printed in its entirety.' ('Man siehet keinen Anschein, daß er jemals werde ganz gedrukt werden.').

Directly following his translation of the first six books of the *Iliad* – an early attempt of adapting the original metric form of Homer's metre, the hexameter – Bodmer printed a text he called '*The Sister's Revenge*.' It is his loose hexametric translation of the last third of the *Nibelungenlied*, the same passage he had singled out for his edition of the Middle High German text a decade earlier.

1767 'Die Ersten Gesänge der Ilias', in [Johann Jakob] Bodmer: *Calliope*, vol. 2. (Zürich), pp. 157–306; *and* 'Die Rache der Schwester', in [Johann Jakob] Bodmer: *Calliope*, vol. 2. (Zürich), pp. 307–72.
Taylor Institution Library: FINCH.U.271

Bodmer continues his ongoing mission of altering the *Nibelungenlied* in order to harmonise it with his ideas about Homer. This involves adding a proem, a form of verse prologue. Styling himself as the singer of another writer's song, Bodmer does not invoke the Muses, goddesses of inspiration. But he alludes to them – to the Greek Muses of Mount Helicon ('Aonien' being a mythical name for Boeotia) as well as to 'German Muses', who used to inspire the poets of the Middle Ages like Wolfram von Eschenbach ('die Eschilbache'). What is more, according to Bodmer's proem, the nameless poet of the *Nibelungenlied* sang 'in the tune' of Homer himself (called 'Mäonides' after his supposed homeland Maeonia or ancestor Maeon).

> Before the Aonian Muses walked in the groves of Germany, when Achilles had not yet fought in German songs and Ulysses not yet deceived the suitors in the guise of a beggar, the Eschilbachs, inspired by German Muses, sang their own songs, the fruit of the spirit that invents on its own. One of them sang, in the tune of Maeonides, about the sister whose dear husband was killed by her brothers; the sister in turn killed the brothers. Time has extinguished his name but preserved his song. I have heard it and intend to sing it louder. It shall resound from the Rhine to the Baltic Sea.
>
> (Eh die aonischen Musen in Deutschlands hainen gewandelt,
> Als Achilles noch nicht in deutschen gesängen gefochten,
> Und Ulysses die freyer noch nicht im bettler betrogen,
> Sangen die Eschilbache, von deutschen Musen begeistert,
> Eigne gesänge, die frucht des selbst erfindenden geistes.
> Einer von ihnen sang mit Mäonides tone die schwester,
> Welcher die brüder den theuen [!] gemahl erschlugen, die schwester
> Wieder die brüder erschlug. Die zeit hat den nahmen getilget,
> Aber sein lied gerettet, ich hab' es gehört, und ich will es
> Lauter singen, es soll vom Rhein zur Ostsee ertönen.)

54 Catalogue

1877 Franz Stolte, 'Der Nibelunge nôt verglichen mit der Ilias. 2. Theil', in *Jahresbericht über das Königliche vollberechtigte Progymnasium Nepomucenum zu Rietberg* (Schuljahr 1876–77), pp. 3–27.
Taylor Institution Library: REP.G.3483 (1–20)

1901 *Das Lied vom Zorn Achills,* aus unserer Ilias hergestellt und in deutsche Nibelungenzeilen übertragen von Julius Schultz, Berlin.
Private loan

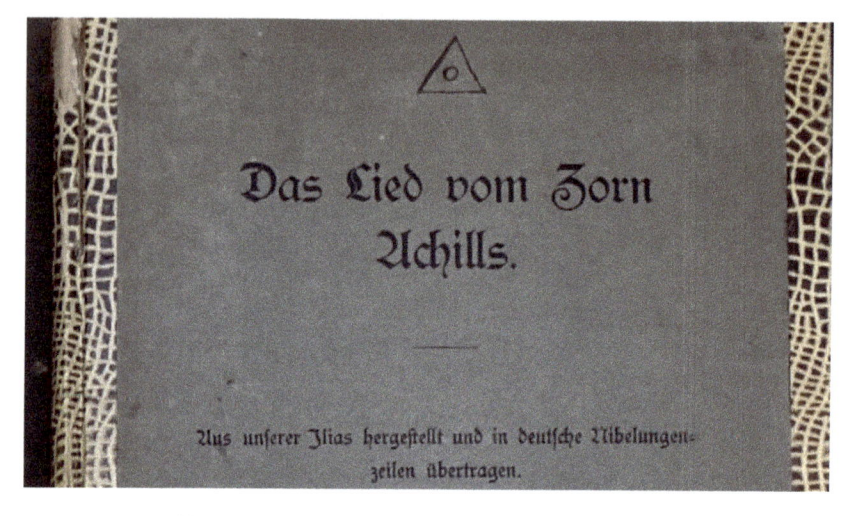

Illustration 12: Censorship mark on Schultz (1901)

The symbol on the cover of a circle or zero inside a triangle was used by the *Oberkommando in den Marken*, a Berlin military authority, to mark books and documents that had passed censorship in World War I. Thanks go to the art historian Holger Birkholz in Dresden, for providing this information.

1986 Bernard Fenik, *Homer and the Nibelungenlied: comparative studies in epic style*, Cambridge, MA.
Taylor Institution Library: EB.610.A.12

2. Translating Verse

Illustration 13: Section 2. From top to bottom: Lord Stanley 1862, Bürger 1776, Voß 1777, Voß 1781, Voß 1780, Voß 1790, Voß/Rupé 1922. Photograph: Philip Flacke

Enthusiasm for the Homeric epics reached new heights in the second half of the eighteenth century, when we come to a new chapter in their German translation. Various young poets, taking their cue from Bodmer and Herder, began work on a German text that was supposed to move its audience in the same way that the original Greek did. To these poets, translation was to a considerable extent a question of metrics. Numerous renderings of extracts of both the *Iliad* and the *Odyssey* were published alongside discussions on prosody and versification, documenting the search for a German Homer.

Earlier critics like Johann Christoph Gottsched had favoured the iambic alexandrine, which followed the literary model of France and had long been supposed to suit the German speech rhythm better than dactyls and spondees. Rejecting the alexandrine in many cases now meant rejecting the exemplary role of French. Gottfried August Bürger explicitly aimed to make Homer 'an old German' ('da ich den Homer in der Übersetzung gleichsam zum alten Deutschen gemacht wissen möchte') and chose iambic pentameter. Friedrich Leopold Stolberg and Johann Heinrich Voss on the other hand, who knew both Bürger and one another from their time at university in Göttingen, aimed to imitate Homer's own metre in German: the hexameter.

Voss went on to publish full translations of the *Odyssey* in 1781 and of the *Iliad* in 1793. His text set a new standard for German writers of hexametric verse in years to come and remains the most influential German translation of Homer to this day. Even a twentieth-century bilingual edition for educated readers like the one in the *Tempel-Klassiker* series presents the German text in a revised version of Voss.

1776 'Homers Iliade. Fünfte Rhapsodie', verdeutscht von Gottfried August Bürger, in *Deutsches Museum* 1776, 1. Stück, pp. 4–14; *and* 'Der Iliade Homers zwanzigster Gesang', verdeutscht durch Friedrich Leopold Graf zu Stolberg, in *Deutsches Museum* 1776, 11. Stück, pp. 957–82.
Taylor Institution Library: VET.PER. 1777

1777 'Odüsseus Erzählung von den Küklopen. Aus dem neunten Gesange der Odüssee Homers', übersetzt von Johann Heinrich Voß, in *Deutsches Museum* 1777, 5. Stück, pp. 462–78.
Taylor Institution Library: VET.PER. 1777

1780 'Ueber Ortügia. Aus dem 15 Ges. der Odüssee' von Johann Heinrich Voß, in *Deutsches Museum* 1780, 4. Stück, pp. 302–12.
Taylor Institution Library: VET.PER. 1780

1781 *Homers Odüßee*, übersetzt von Johann Heinrich Voß, Hamburg.
Private loan

1790 'Probe der Vossischen Ilias', [translated by Johann Heinrich Voß], in *Neues Deutsches Museum* 2, 1. Stück, pp. 1–43.
Taylor Institution Library: VET.PER. Bd.2 (1790: Jan./Jun.)

1862 [Edward Smith-Stanley, 14th Earl of Derby], *Translations of Poems, Ancient and Modern Not Published*, London.
Taylor Institution Library: FIEDLER.A.150

Lord Stanley is the only British Prime Minister so far to have translated Homer's *Iliad*. His take on its first book is included in this volume, of which, according to the dedication, only a few copies were printed for friends. On his choice of metre he writes 'that, if justice is ever to be done to the easy flow and majestic simplicity of the grand old Poet, it can only be in the heroic blank verse'. He writes more extensively on the matter in the preface to his full translation of the *Iliad* that was to follow two years later and appeared in several editions:

> Numerous as have been the translators of the Iliad, or of parts of it, the metres which have been selected have been almost as various: the ordinary couplet in rhyme, the Spenserian stanza, the Trochaic or Ballad metre, all have had their partisans, even to that 'pestilent heresy' of the so-called English Hexameter; a metre wholly repugnant to the genius of our language; which can only be pressed into the service by a violation of every rule of prosody; and of which, notwithstanding my respect for the eminent men who have attempted to naturalize it, I could never read ten lines without being

irresistibly reminded of Canning's 'Dactylics call'st thou them? God help thee, silly one!'

1861 *Homer's Gedichte*, im Versmaße der Urschrift übersetzt von Karl Uschner, in zwei Theilen, erster Theil: Ilias, zweiter Theil: Odyssee, Berlin.
Taylor Institution Library: 1.B.21 (two volumes in one)

While Lord Stanley might have deemed the 'English hexameter' a 'pestilent heresy', the German Karl Uschner undertook a new translation of Homer 'in the original metre' – which is to say, in hexameter. Nonetheless, Uschner seems to reflect on differences between German and Homer's Ionic Greek in a *distichon*, two lines of verse in which a pentameter follows a hexameter, redolent of *captatio benevolentiae*, a rhetorical technique to ensure goodwill:

> Deinen ionischen nahn germanische Laute mit Zagheit;
> Sei, Ermunterer, Du Deinem Ermunterten hold!
> (German sounds approach your Ionic ones timidly. You who encourage others, be charitable with the one you encouraged!)

1902 *Das alte Lied vom Zorne Achills (Urmenis)*, aus der *Ilias* ausgeschieden und metrisch übersetzt von August Fick, Göttingen.
Taylor Institution Library: 2931 e.46

The book is an attempt to identify the supposedly oldest parts of the *Iliad*, its 'primordial core' ('Urkern') according to certain numerical principles. By eliminating all the (allegedly) later additions to the text, thus shortening it to only 1936 verses, and by then translating these verses into German, Fick aims to make Homer accessible to school children. Fick's view is that the epic is too long to be enjoyed in its entirety:

> The *Iliad* [...] is composed of 15,639 verses! This begs the question how such an amount, which prevents any novel pleasure, could have come into being.
> (Die Ilias [...] besteht aus 15,693 Versen! Da fragt es sich, wie ein solcher allen frischen Genuß ausschließender Umfang entstanden sein kann.)

[1922] *Homers Ilias*, auf Grund der Übersetzungen von Johann Heinrich Voß verdeutscht von Hans Rupé, vol. 1: Erster bis zwölfter Gesang, Berlin/Leipzig.
Taylor Institution Library: REP.G.7250

3. Mapping Myth

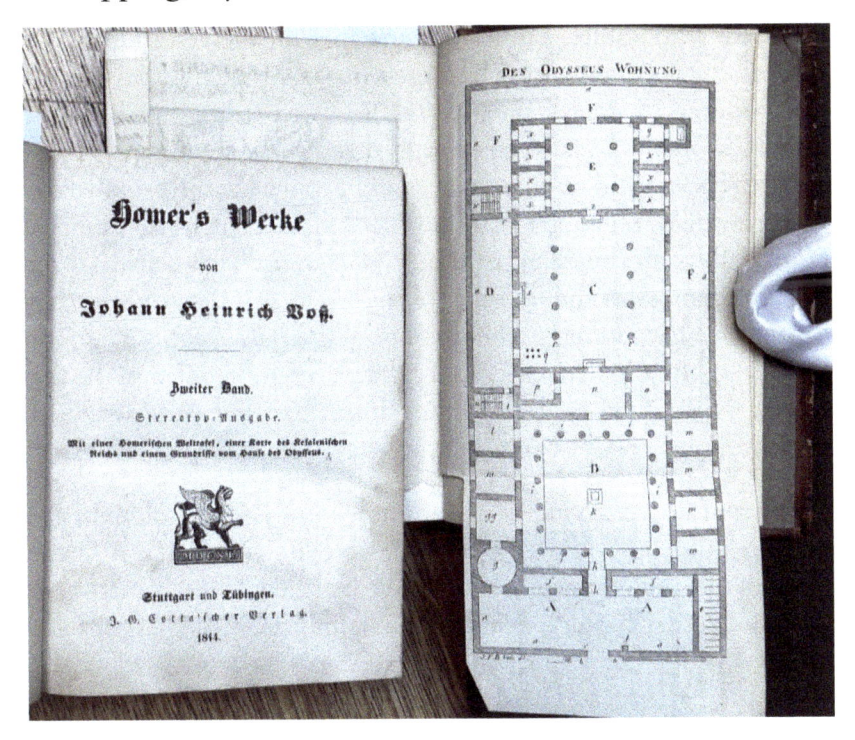

Illustration 14: The House of Odysseus (Voß 1844). Photograph: Philip Flacke

The Homeric epics and the *Nibelungenlied* each situate characters and action in a complex topography, mixing real place names and landmarks with imaginary and mythical spheres. This combination of historical events and characters with the ahistorical and the fantastic means that the narratives make it impossible to draw a line between fact and fiction. It may be precisely for this reason that locating the epics in the real world plays such an important role in the reception of both Homer and the *Nibelungenlied*. The tip of this iceberg could be the popular desire to discover the legendary treasure of the *Nibelungenhort* at the bottom of the Rhine, much like Schliemann in the 1870s when he claimed to have excavated Priam's Treasure. This was a major plot point in a 2023 episode of *Tatort* situated in Ludwigshafen am Rhein and entitled 'Gold'.

A number of maps and plans are included in an 1844 edition of Voss' *Iliad* and *Odyssey*, amongst them a plan of Odysseus' house in Ithaca complete with stables, kennel, and the spot for the vessels in which wine and water are mixed. The largest map shows the world according to Homer. It depicts the Mediterranean according to the outline shown on modern maps, but within this realistic topography it includes fictitious and mythical places and people like the cannibalistic Laestrygonians on an island in the Alboran Sea. A school edition of Franz Fühmann's retelling of the *Nibelungenlied* adds a map to the text that represents the 'Journey of the legendary Burgundians/Nibelungs [...] according to the account of the *Nibelungenlied* (around 1200 AD)'. Again, fictitious events and places are situated in the real world: '*Nibelungenhort* sunk in the Rhine', 'Etzel's castle: demise of the Nibelungs'. A German forest serves as backdrop.

A different way of trying to orient oneself in the world of myth can be seen in a copy of Gustav Schwab's retellings of Ancient Greek myth in the Taylorian collection. In the margins and on blank pages, a former reader has drawn numerous family trees of the gods and heroes described by Homer and his successors.

1844 *Homer's Werke* von Johann Heinrich Voß, Stereotyp-Ausgabe, erster Band, mit einer Karte von Troja, Stuttgart/Tübingen.
Taylor Institution Library: 52.A.1

1844 *Homer's Werke* von Johann Heinrich Voß, Stereotyp-Ausgabe, zweiter Band, mit einer Homerischen Welttafel, einer Karte des Kefalenischen Reichs und einem Grundrisse vom Hause des Odysseus, Stuttgart/Tübingen.
Taylor Institution Library: 52.A.1.A

1882 Gustav Schwab, *Die schönsten Sagen des klassischen Alterthums. Nach seinen Dichtern und Erzählern*, mit 8 Holzschnitten, 14th edition, Gütersloh/Leipzig.
Taylor Institution Library: MONTGOMERY.5.B.11

Section 3: Mapping Myth   61

*Illustration 15: Section 3. From top to bottom, left to right:
Fry 2020, Mudrak 1955, Bartsch/de Boor 1988, Voß 1844, Fühmann 2005.
Photograph: Philip Flacke*

62 Catalogue

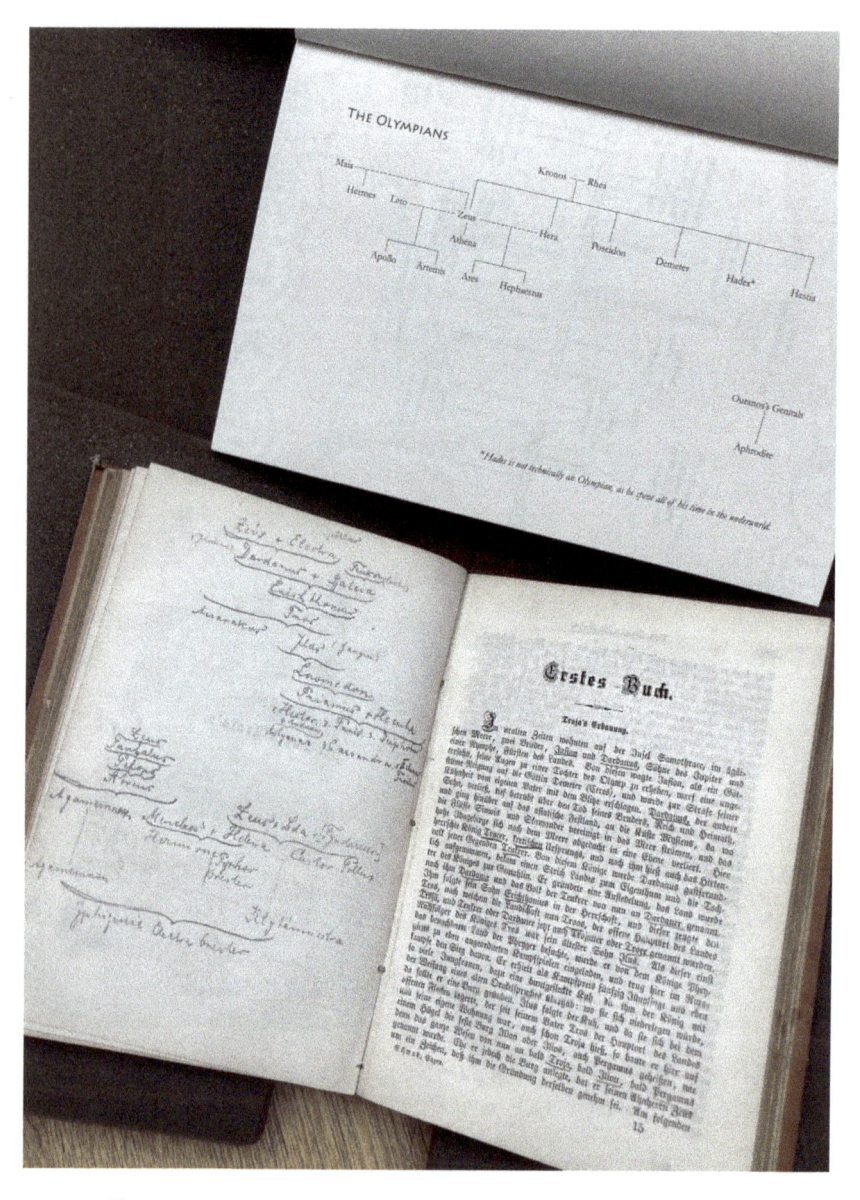

*Illustration 16: Section 3. Top: Fry 2020, bottom: Schwab 1882.
Photograph: Philip Flacke*

1955 *Deutsche Heldensagen*, herausgegeben von Edmund Mudrak, Reutlingen. Private loan

Mudrak, an Austrian ethnologist, filled various positions in Nazi Germany, gaining influence on both cultural and educational matters, and became professor at the University of Posen in occupied Poland in 1943. After the Second World War, Mudrak went on to publish a number of popular retellings of supposedly 'Germanic' myths, like this one, which builds on the popular book *Germanischer Sagenborn* (originally *Germania's Sagenborn* 1889/90) by the German author Emil Engelmann. Despite his political background, some of Mudrak's retellings are still in print.

1988 *Das Nibelungenlied*, nach der Ausgabe von Karl Bartsch herausgegeben von Helmut de Boor, 22. revidierte und von Roswitha Wisniewski ergänzte Auflage, Mannheim (Deutsche Klassiker des Mittelalters). Private loan

Helmut de Boor took over revising Bartsch's classic edition of the *Nibelungenlied* while being an active member of the Nazi Party, with the 10th edition coming out in 1940. He was dismissed from his position at the University of Bern in 1945 but took up the Chair at the Freie Universität Berlin, and became one of the most influential medievalists of post-war Germany.

1993 Franz Fühmann, *Der Nibelunge Not. Szenarium für einen Spielfilm*, mit einem Nachwort von Peter Göhler, Berlin.
Taylor Institution Library: SD.2682.A.1

2005 *Das Nibelungenlied*, neu erzählt von Franz Fühmann, mit Materialien, zusammengestellt von Isolde Schnabel, Stuttgart/Leipzig (Taschenbücherei Texte & Materialien). Private loan

2020 Stephen Fry, *Troy*, London.
Bodleian Library: XWeek 51 (20)

4. Powerful Women

*Illustration 17: Section 4. From top to bottom, left to right:
Cross 2012, Lang n.d., Neureuther 1843, Otto 1903, Draesner 2016.
Photograph: Philip Flacke*

Section 4: Powerful Women 65

*Illustration 18: Section 4. From top to bottom, left to right:
Anon. 1907, Hoepke 1975, MacGregor 1908, Lamb 1926.
Photograph: Philip Flacke*

The stories of Homer and the *Nibelungenlied* have had a firm place in the canons of both adult and children's literature for generations.

This has meant a more or less constant demand for illustrated editions, popular retellings, and adaptations in simple language. While scholarly translations were historically done by men (the first women to translate the *Iliad* and the *Odyssey* into English being Caroline Alexander in 2015 and Emily Wilson in 2017 and 2023), women played an important part in adaptations for children.

Even if one excludes Homer's Olympian goddesses, who do not strictly have counterparts in the *Nibelungenlied*, various protagonists in all of these epics are both powerful and female. The illustrators depict them in various ways, sometimes with surprising similarities. There is surely some resemblance in the majestic postures and commanding gestures of both Circe and Brünhild, the one transforming Odysseus' men into pigs in a design by Friedrich Preller, reused for the 1903 edition of Helene Otto, the other ordering Kriemhild to stand still and stay behind in a design by Carl Otto Czeschka, reused in Ulrike Draesner's 2016 edition of the *Nibelungenlied*? Other illustrations differ in ways which tell us something about the underlying ideas of femininity and power. Are Brünhild and Circe depicted in their moments of superiority, or only when subdued by male heroes? Do they more resemble queens or witches? Are they sexualised and in what way?

1843 Gustav Pfizer, *Der Nibelungen Noth*, illustriert mit Holzschnitten nach Zeichnungen von Julius Schnorr von Carolsfeld und Eugen Neureuther, Stuttgart/Tübingen. Taylor Institution Library: 38.M.13

This verse translation of the *Nibelungenlied* into modern German had an enduring legacy because of its visual layout. It includes a large number of woodcuts produced by the Xylographische Anstalt von Kaspar Braun & [Georg] von Dessauer, based on illustrations by Julius Schnorr von Carolsfeld and Eugen Neureuther. Beginning in the 1820s, Schnorr created a series of frescoes to decorate the walls and ceilings of a series of rooms in the royal palace of King Ludwig I in Munich, and these had a second life as woodcuts. The woodcuts, as included by Pfizer, along with the related page design, found their way directly into a number of other *Nibelungenlied* translations, and were enormously influential for further *Nibelungenlied* translators and adapters.

Section 4: Powerful Women 67

1903 *Odyssee,* in der Sprache der Zehnjährigen erzählt von Helene Otto, mit 10 Vollbildern von Friedrich Preller und einer Vorrede an Eltern, Lehrer und Erzieher von B[erthold] Otto, Leipzig. Private loan

In the 'preface for parents, educators, and teachers', the German pedagogue Berthold Otto explains the educational value of, as the title says, a retelling of Homer 'in the language of ten-year-olds': Making sure children could actually understand what they were reading was meant to prevent an empty verbosity ('hohle Phrasenhaftigkeit') that they might otherwise acquire. The violence is not scaled down however which, when the story is told in childish words, has an unsettling effect – as for example in the punishment of the maids and the goatherd Melanthius: 'When everything was finished, they (Telemachus and the two herdsmen) brought the maids into the courtyard and hanged them all one after the other. Then they took Melanthius and cut off his nose and then his ears, and they broke his arms and legs so they were in pieces.' ('Als alles fertig war, führten sie (Telemach und die beiden Hirten) die Mägde in den Hof und hängten sie alle der Reihe nach auf. Dann nahmen sie den Melantheus und schnitten ihm die Nase und die Ohren ab und brachen ihm Arme und Beine kaput.') The only omission is Melanthius' castration. (That his limbs are being broken instead of his hands and feet being cut off, is arguably a minor change.)

All the reader learns about the author of the book is that she was 'the teller of fairy tales and myths for her younger siblings and their playmates from earliest youth'. In fact, Helene Otto was Berthold's oldest daughter and only about 16 years when the book was published. (The text had already been published in her father's periodical 'Der Hauslehrer'.) In the course of one year after the publication of her *Odyssey,* there followed five retellings of canonical narratives by Helene Otto in the language of ten- or eight-year-olds, including two volumes on the Nibelungen myth and a version of the *Iliad.*

1907 Anonymous, *The Linden Leaf; or, The Story of Siegfried. Retold from the Nibelungen Lied*, London. Taylor Institution Library: 28849 f.4

This is another publication aimed at a young audience that includes eight brightly coloured illustrations, which seem to be signed 'Waugh'. It adapts the first half of the *Nibelungenlied,* also making brief reference to some other legends of Siegfried's youth. It ends after Siegfried's murder and, although it alludes to Kriemhild's desire to 'punish his murderer', there is no more explicit reference to her vengeance, and readers are assured that Hagen ultimately meets a hero's death, having 'fully atoned for his sins'.

1908 Mary MacGregor, *Stories of Siegfried, told to the children*, with pictures by Granville Fell, London/New York. Private loan

Unusually, this children's adaptation does not appeal to a shared Germanic heritage, but draws a distinction between 'the German hero', Siegfried, and 'your French and English heroes'. MacGregor draws on Norse material to an extent, but her primary source is the first half of the *Nibelungenlied*. She deals with the second half of the narrative in the final page, noting that Siegfried's death was eventually 'avenged by Queen Kriemhild', but implies that the violence was carried out only by men, and omits Kriemhild's own fate. There are eight colour plates by Granville Fell. The publication is undated, but 1908 is the usual date given. The exhibition features two other books from this series: *Stories from the Odyssey* and *Stories from the Iliad*.

[n.d.] Jeanie Lang, *Stories from the Odyssey, told to the children*, with pictures by W. Heath Robinson, London/Edinburgh. Private loan

This children's adaptation is part of the same 'Told to the children' series as *Stories of Siegfried* and *Stories from the Iliad*. The early-twentieth-century endeavour aimed to retell stories deemed to represent the western canon in language appropriate for 9-12 year-olds.

1926 Charles Lamb, *The Adventures of Ulysses*, with Illustrations by Doris Pailthorpe and T. H. Robinson, London et al.
Bodleian Library: 2527 e.819/20c

1975 *Homers Odyssee*, neu gefaßt von Hermann Hoepke mit 15 Linolschnitten von Hella Ackermann, Baden-Baden/Brüssel/Köln. Private loan

2012 Homer, *The Iliad and the Odyssey*, retold by Gillian Cross, with Illustrations by Neil Packer, London. Bodleian Library: XWeek 13 (18)

2016 Ulrike Draesner, *Nibelungen. Heimsuchung*, mit den Illustrationen von Carl Otto Czeschka, Stuttgart.
Taylor Institution Library: PT2664.R324 N53 DRA 2016

5. The Pierced Body

*Illustration 19: Section 5. From top to bottom, left to right:
Lang n.d., Otto 1904, Wägner/Heichen 1943, Cartwright 1907, Marbach 1840.
Photograph: Philip Flacke*

70 Catalogue

*Illustration 20: Section 5. From top to bottom, left to right:
Picard 1986, Hoepke 1977, Green 1974, Green 1965.
Photograph: Philip Flacke*

Section 5: The Pierced Body

Blood springs forth in a high arch from the gaping wound of a dying Trojan. A spear is thrust through a man's neck. Siegfried sinks down looking at the weapon that protrudes from his chest. Simply put, these pictures – the majority of which appeared in children's books – spotlight violence. They showcase the severed body having been, or about to be, pierced by a weapon, and that weapon is always present. Two illustrations, by W. Heath Robinson and Betty Middleton-Sandford, do not actually depict stab wounds but show the dead lying beside the weapon that killed them. And yet everything appears to be clean. No dirt, no crusted blood stains the fabrics, spears, or shields; the plumed helmets look impeccable. How much do these pictures still inform our ideas of masculine heroism?

The stabbing of Siegfried was given ideological significance by right-wing German forces after the First World War. In a committee inquiring into the causes, prolongation, and loss of the war, the future Reichspräsident Paul von Hindenburg claimed to the German parliament that the German forces had been 'stabbed in the back'. With this historical lie, Hindenburg, who had himself been partly responsible for the military action, put the blame on democratic and socialist groups in Germany. These were claimed to have sabotaged the 'heroic' endeavours of the military. The 'Dolchstoßlegende' ('stab-in-the-back myth') was incorporated into right-wing narratives, quickly gaining antisemitic overtones, and was heavily used as propaganda by the Nazi party.

The *Nibelungenlied* made an abstract idea concrete in both text and image. Siegfried, who like Achilles can only be wounded on a single specific spot on his body, is murdered as he is lying down to drink from a spring. Hagen, vassal to his brother-in-law, stabs him from behind with his own spear. Hindenburg and others were ready to cast the German forces in the role of Siegfried, an almost invulnerable hero who could only have been brought down by treacherous deceit. In the course of this, the spear of the *Nibelungenlied* became the prototypical backstabbing weapon: a dagger (the 'Dolch' part of the 'Dolchstoß'). The image of the 'Dolchstoß' served as an essential component in the project of linking the *Nibelungen* to national identity. This is emphasised in a 1943 edition of *Germanic Tales about Gods and Heroes* (*Germanische Götter- und Heldensagen*), which shows a still from Fritz Lang's two-part film series *Die Nibelungen* (1924) as its frontispiece.

1840 *Das Nibelungenlied*. Uebersetzt von Gotthard Oswald Marbach, mit Holzschnitten nach Originalzeichnungen von Eduard Bendemann und Julius Hübner, Denkmal zur vierten Säcularfeier der Buchdruckerkunst, Leipzig. Private loan

Gotthard Oswald Marbach was Richard Wagner's brother-in-law and an associate professor at the University of Leipzig. Beginning in 1838, he issued a sprawling series of *Volksbücher* over a relatively short number of years, often intervening dramatically in the material – though he appears to have been relatively careful with the *Nibelungenlied*. Other German translators of medieval literature, in particular Karl Simrock, held Marbach in low regard. As a work of *Druckkunst*, the art of printing, however, this book was a dramatic statement of what could be accomplished in the interaction of text and image.

1904 *Ilias*, in der Sprache der Zehnjährigen erzählt von Helene Otto, mit 6 Vollbildern von C[arl] Bertling, Leipzig. Private loan

Helene Otto's *Iliad* claims the same naturalistic authenticity as her *Odyssey* a year earlier. 'Of course, you all know that you're not supposed to write like this in an essay. But here everything is written down and printed as it is actually spoken.' ('Ihr wißt natürlich alle, daß man so im Aufsatz nicht schreiben darf. Aber hier ist alles so aufgeschrieben und gedruckt, wie es wirklich gesprochen wird.') So goes a footnote explaining why the preposition *wegen* is colloquially used with dative instead of genitive. Again, the child-like language contrasts sharply with the violent action – as in the description of the scene depicted here (cf. *Il.* 11, 451–479). The recurring phrase *totmachen* for 'kill' is hard to translate. Literally meaning 'to make dead', it lends the register of the very young to a brutal action.

> At last, he also struck dead a very brave Trojan. Then his brother came. He said to Odysseus: 'Either you are dead or I am dead.' At once, he threw his lance at him. The lance went through the shield

Section 5: The Pierced Body 73

and through the armour and cut Odysseus' skin. Then, Pallas Athena stopped the lance so that the lance wouldn't kill Odysseus. Odysseus realised that he wasn't wounded so very badly that he would die. Then, he threw his lance after the one who had wounded him, and he struck him between his shoulders because he had wanted to run away and had turned round.

(Zuletzt schlug er auch noch einen sehr tapferen Troer tot. Da kam dem sein Bruder. Der sagte zu Odysseus: 'Entweder du machst mich tot, oder ich mach dich tot.' Dabei warf er nach ihm mit der Lanze. Die Lanze ging durch den Schild durch und durch den Panzer durch und ritzte dem Odysseus die Haut. Dann hielt Pallas Athene die Lanze auf, damit die Lanze den Odysseus nicht tot machte. Odysseus merkte, daß er noch nicht so sehr schlimm verwundet war, daß er sterben mußte. Er warf nun seine Lanze nach dem, der ihn verwundet hatte, und er traf ihn zwischen die Schultern, denn der hatte ausreißen wollen und hatte sich dazu umgedreht.)

According to inscriptions on the front endpapers, both copies of Otto's Homer retellings shown in the exhibition used to belong to a book collection owned by the 'Elternbund der deutschen Erneuerungsgemeinde'. Founded in 1904, the 'Deutsche Erneuerungs-Gemeinde' ('German community for renewal') aimed to establish settlements in rural Brandenburg built on ideas of racial purity and Germanic 'land-right', an antisemitic world view, and anti-modern resentment.

[n.d.] Jeanie Lang, *Stories from the Iliad; or, The Siege of Troy, told to the children*, with pictures by W. Heath Robinson, London/New York.
Private loan

This children's adaptation is part of the same 'Told to the children' series as *Stories of Siegfried* and *Stories from the Odyssey* (above). This was an early-twentieth-century endeavour which aimed to retell stories deemed to represent the western canon in language appropriate for 9-12 year-olds.

1907 Tho[ma]s Cartwright, *Sigurd the Dragon-Slayer. A Twice-Told Tale*, London (Every Child's Library).
Bodleian Library: 930 f.107

Cartwright offers a retelling for children, first of the Norse material 'as fashioned ... for the delight of our sea-roving Viking forefathers', and then of the *Nibelungenlied*, 'for which we are indebted to our cousins, the Germans'. The text of the latter section is taken entirely from Thomas Carlyle. In addition to eight colour plates, there are numerous black and white engravings. No details are given for the illustrator(s), but some of the black and white images are accompanied by the monogram 'I.B.'. It does not appear that on this occasion Cartwright worked with Patten Wilson, who illustrated his *Brave Beowulf* in the same series. In a preamble intended to appear handwritten, Cartwright invokes William Morris's comparison of the *Nibelungen* material to the Homeric epics.

1943 *Walhalla. Germanische Götter- und Heldensagen*, nach den hochdeutschen Fassungen von Simrock und Wägner bearbeitet von Walter Heichen, Berlin. Private loan

1965 *The Tale of Troy*, retold from the Ancient authors by Roger Lancelyn Green, illustrated by Betty Middleton-Sandford, London. Private loan

1974 *The Tale of Troy*, retold from the Ancient authors by Roger Lancelyn Green, illustrated by Pauline Baynes, London. Private loan

1977 *Homers Ilias*, neugefaßt von Hermann Hoepke mit 13 Holzschnitten von Hella Ackermann, Baden-Baden/Köln/New York. Private loan

1986 *The Iliad & Odyssey of Homer*, retold for children by Barbara Leonie Picard, illustrated by Joan Kiddel-Monroe, Oxford (The Oxford Children's Classics). Bodleian Library: 25398 e.3747

6. Violent Revenge

*Illustration 21: Section 6. From top to bottom, left to right:
Church 1907, Mackenzie 1912, Hands 1880,
Agrimbau/Klassen 2018 (Odyssey), Colum 1920, Atwood 2018.
Photograph: Philip Flacke*

76 Catalogue

*Illustration 22: Section 6. From top to bottom, left to right:
Church 1908, Anon. 1911, Agrimbau/Klassen 2018 (Iliad), Hands 1880,
Miller 2011, Picard 1986 (for the last see section 5).
Photograph: Philip Flacke*

Section 6: Violent Revenge

Both the *Odyssey* and the *Nibelungenlied* end in bloodbath: The disguised Odysseus, coming home to his wife Penelope and his son Telemachus twenty years after he set off for Troy, finds his house full of suitors who eat and drink at his expense and want to marry his supposed widow. He finally traps them in his hall and kills them all with the help of Telemachus and two herdsmen. Twelve maids, whom Odysseus believes to have been disloyal to him, are forced to clean up the blood of the suitors and are then hanged on Odysseus' command. Margaret Atwood in her 2005 novella *The Penelopiad* gives the twelve maids the role of a Greek choir, giving them the chance to speak for themselves and comment on events.

Like Odysseus, Kriemhild orders the slaughter of those upon whom she wants to take vengeance. At her invitation, the Burgundians, whom she holds responsible for the death of her first husband Siegfried, come to the castle of her second husband, Etzel. There, they are all killed in the feasting hall. The slaughter of the suitors and the slaughter of the Burgundians are depicted in ways that share some similar features. For one, the heroes appear above a pile of corpses. But where do the similarities end? With whom is the viewer supposed to sympathise, if at all? Is the violence imagined as just? Is it glorified or abhorred, downplayed or celebrated?

Kriemhild herself takes part in the violence, transgressing both medieval and Victorian gender roles. At one point, she appears before Hagen holding the decapitated head of her brother and his former king. She will imminently go on to decapitate another man, this time with her own hands, and it will be Hagen. This scene often features in illustration, including in Lydia Hands' *Nibelungenlied* adaptation 'for the use of young readers', which reuses the designs by Julius Schnorr von Carolsfeld and Eugen Neureuther, mediated through their slightly revised appearance in one of Karl Simrock's *Nibelungenlied* translations. Children's versions of the *Iliad*, too, sometimes depict the mutilated dead body – or rather, the public desecration of a corpse that by divine intervention cannot be mutilated. In Helene Otto's *Odyssey* for ten-year-olds, Achilles can be seen on a chariot dragging Hector's corpse around the walls of Troy to avenge the death of his lover Patroclus. Madeline Miller's 2011 novel *The Song of Achilles* tells the story of Achilles and Patroclus as a queer reading of the *Iliad*.

1880 Lydia Hands, *Golden Threads from an Ancient Loom. Das Nibelunglied*, adapted to the use of young readers, with fourteen wood engravings by Julius Schnorr, of Carolsfeld, London/New York. Private loan

Golden Threads is the first of the flood of children's adaptations of *Nibelungen*-related material in the later nineteenth and early twentieth centuries. It is unusually complete amongst works aimed at children in adapting the full narrative, albeit with some obfuscation. The narrative was augmented with additional legends of Siegfried, all found in Thomas Carlyle's essay, and Carlyle was the dedicatee. The woodcuts and the corresponding layout are a selection from those which originally appeared in Pfizer's *Der Nibelungen Noth* (1843), though Hands discovered them in, and reproduced them from, a translation by Karl Simrock, published in 1873. She casts Kriemhild as driven to violence by madness – an excuse for violent women also used in legal contexts.

1897 Margaret Armour, *The Fall of the Nibelungs*, illustrated and decorated by W.B. MacDougall, London.
Taylor Institution Library: FIEDLER.G.600

Armour's *Fall of the Nibelungs* is relatively unusual amongst complete translations of the *Nibelungenlied* into English in being illustrated – and her illustrator was her husband. It was more common for illustrations to appear in adaptations. Translators were often overtly concerned to present their work as scholarly, and this was often taken to preclude images. Armour intended her translation to be a close rendering of the medieval text in modern English prose, and it was well received as such. Like most nineteenth-century anglophone translators, however, she also made use of a modern German translation, in this case a parallel text edition by Karl Simrock, which offered access to the Middle High German alongside a modern German text.

1907 *The Children's Odyssey*, told from Homer in simple language by Alfred J. Church, with twelve ills, London. Bodleian Library: 2932 e.39

1908 *The Children's Iliad.*, told from Homer in simple language by Alfred J. Church, with twelve illustrations, London.
Bodleian Library: 2931 e.52

1911 Anonymous, *Siegfried and Kriemhild. A Story of Passion and Revenge*, illustrated by Frank C. Papé, London et al. (The World's Romances).
Bodleian Library: 28849 d.25

This is a relatively thorough retelling of the *Nibelungenlied* for children, with the framing device that it is told in a tavern in Worms in 1460. The Kriemhild of this adaptation is ultimately even more violent than the medieval Kriemhild, killing her brother, as well as Hagen, herself, but the author follows Lydia Hands in implying that her actions are the result of madness. The text is accompanied by eight colour plates by Frank Cheyne Papé (1878–1972).

1912 Donald Mackenzie, *Teutonic Myths and Legend. An Introduction to the Edday & Sagas, Beowulf, The Nibelungenlied, etc.*, London.
Bodleian Library: 930 e.541

Mackenzie's collection of shortened retellings described itself as 'an introduction to the *Eddas* and Sagas, *Beowulf*, The *Nibelungenlied*. etc.'. It was aimed at adults and, like other similar publications, included a number of images previously published elsewhere. The image displayed is based on one of Julius Schnorr von Carolsfeld's frescoes – and notably not a woodcut version. The publication is undated, but 1912 is the usual date given.

1920 Padraic Colum, *The Adventures of Odysseus and the Tale of Troy*, presented [=illustrated] by Willy Pogány, London.
Bodleian Library: 2932 e.53

2011 Madeline Miller, *The Song of Achilles*, London et al.
Bodleian Library: XWeek 36 (11)

2018 Diego Agrimbau and Smilton Roa Klassen, *Homer's The Iliad. A Graphic Novel*, Oxford. Bodleian Library: XWeek 35 (17)

2018 Diego Agrimbau and Smilton Roa Klassen, *Homer's The Odyssey. A Graphic Novel*, Oxford. Bodleian Library: XWeek 35 (17)

2018 Margaret Atwood, *The Penelopiad*, Edinburgh (Canons/The Myths). Private loan

2020 Playmobil 70469 – *Achilles and Patroclus with Chariot*, plastic toy figures, Zirndorf. Private loan

The toy figures of Achilles and Patroclus, sold by a company in Bavaria, are part of a series with sets of different characters from Greek myth. According to the manufacturer, they are aimed at four- to ten-year-olds. On the Playmobil website, Achilles and Patroclus are introduced not as lovers but as 'friends since childhood', always standing 'side by side in battle'. Children are then encouraged to reenact Patroclus' death and Achilles avenging him in his battle against Hector – notwithstanding Hector not being included in the set: 'But one day Patroclus puts on Achilles' armour and rides into battle alone. There he is killed by Hector, the prince of Troy, who mistakenly believes him to be Achilles. Achilles is furious about the death of his friend and sets out to avenge him and kill Hector.' Although Playmobil has produced toy versions of a number of men who serve as key figures in German national identity – Dürer, Luther, Bach, Goethe, Schiller –, there are no sets based on the *Nibelungenlied*.

Section 6: Violent Revenge   81

Illustration 23: Playmobil set for section 6. In the background, left to right:
Lang n.d. (section 5), Colum 1920 (section 6), Church 1908 (section 6);
under the horses: Green 1965 (section 5).
Photograph: Philip Flacke

Bodleian Library: Homeric Fragments curated by NIGEL WILSON and PETER TÓTH

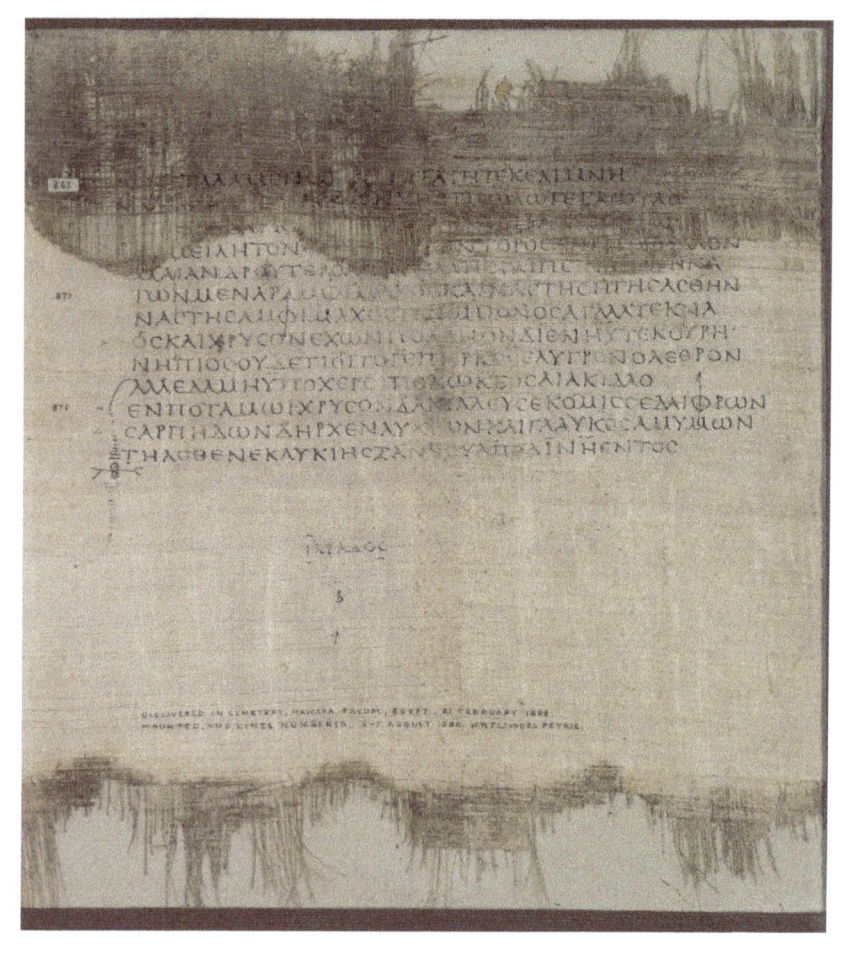

Illustration 24: The Hawara Homer. End of Book 2

Homeric Fragments

1. Bodleian Library, MS. Gr. class. a. 1(P)/1-10 = p. Hawara (c. 150), papyrus.
   https://medieval.bodleian.ox.ac.uk/catalog/manuscript_4977

This papyrus, the 'Hawara Homer', dating from the second century A.D., contains part of *Iliad* Book 2. It is noteworthy for the use of marginal signs invented by Alexandrian scholars to indicate lines that should be deleted or were thought to raise other points of interest.

2. Bodleian Library, MS. Auct. V. 1. 51. (late 10th cent.), parchment.
   https://medieval.bodleian.ox.ac.uk/catalog/manuscript_874

The Homeric poems retained their place in the school curriculum, but linguistic changes posed an increasingly difficult problem for the pupils. This MS, probably written at the turn of the tenth and eleventh centuries, is a glossary for readers of the *Odyssey*. It is far from certain that the average pupil could afford such a book, and this one probably belonged to a relatively well-off schoolmaster.

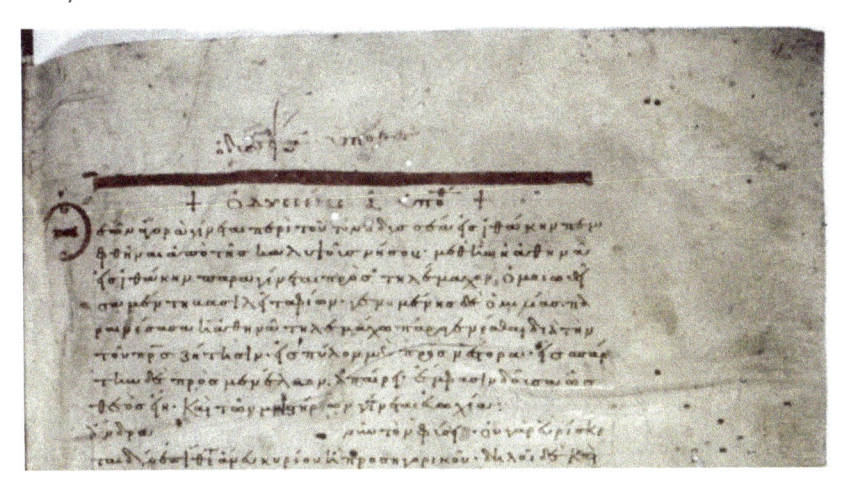

Illustration 25: Bodleian Library, MS. Auct. V. 1. 51., fol. 1r. The text shown here is a synopsis of Book 1 of the Odyssey

3. Bodleian Library, MS. Auct. T. 2. 7 (12th cent.), parchment.
https://medieval.bodleian.ox.ac.uk/catalog/manuscript_784

A copy of the *Iliad*, probably from the early twelfth century, with extensive marginalia, mostly paraphrase. The script is rather cursive.

4. Bodleian Library, MS. Laud gr. 54 (early 15th cent.), paper.
https://medieval.bodleian.ox.ac.uk/catalog/manuscript_6866

This copy of the *Iliad* from the early fifteenth century contains Books 1-2 only. The limited content could be regarded as a sign of drastic reduction of the curriculum, of which there is other evidence.

5. Bodleian Library, MS. Canonici gr. 43 (16th cent.), paper.
https://medieval.bodleian.ox.ac.uk/catalog/manuscript_2477

This is a 16th-century copy of *Iliad* Books 1–10. Though the text had been printed in Florence in 1488 and by Aldus in 1504 hand-written copies continued to be produced.

5. Bodleian Library, MS. Canonici gr. 79 (early 16th cent.), paper.
https://medieval.bodleian.ox.ac.uk/catalog/manuscript_2509

Ilias Latina (*Epitome Iliadis*)

6. Bodleian Library, Auct. F. 2.14, fol. 90r (12th cent.), parchment.
https://medieval.bodleian.ox.ac.uk/catalog/manuscript_610

This miscellany includes the *Ilias Latina*. It was probably produced in the second half of the twelfth century, perhaps at Winchester or Sherborne.

7. Bodleian Library, MS. Rawlinson G. 57 (12th cent.), parchment.
https://medieval.bodleian.ox.ac.uk/catalog/manuscript_8593

Another twelfth-century miscellany containing the *Ilias Latina*.

Illustration 26: 'myths retold' display at Blackwell's Bookshop, Broad Street Oxford, in May 2024. Photograph: Philip Flacke

Milton Keynes UK
Ingram Content Group UK Ltd.
UKHW021810050724
444977UK00007B/24